TREATS FROM

little and friday.

Kim Evans

Photography by Rene Vaile

PENGUIN BOOKS

PENGUIN BOOKS
Published by the Penguin Group
Penguin Group (NZ), 67 Apollo Drive, Rosedale,
Auckland 0632, New Zealand (a division of Pearson New Zealand Ltd)
Penguin Group (USA) Inc., 375 Hudson Street,
New York, New York 10014, USA
Penguin Group (Canada), 90 Eglinton Avenue East, Suite 700, Toronto,
Ontario, M4P 2Y3, Canada (a division of Pearson Penguin Canada Inc.)
Penguin Books Ltd, 80 Strand, London, WC2R 0RL, England
Penguin Ireland, 25 St Stephen's Green,
Dublin 2, Ireland (a division of Penguin Books Ltd)
Penguin Group (Australia), 250 Camberwell Road, Camberwell,
Victoria 3124, Australia (a division of Pearson Australia Group Pty Ltd)
Penguin Books India Pvt Ltd, 11, Community Centre,
Panchsheel Park, New Delhi – 110 017, India
Penguin Books (South Africa) (Pty) Ltd, 24 Sturdee Avenue,
Rosebank, Johannesburg 2196, South Africa

Penguin Books Ltd, Registered Offices: 80 Strand, London, WC2R 0RL,
England

First published by Penguin Group (NZ), 2012
5 6 7 8 9 10

Copyright © Kim Evans, 2012

The right of Kim Evans to be identified as the author of this work in
terms of section 96 of the Copyright Act 1994 is hereby asserted.

Designed and typeset by Anna Egan-Reid, © Penguin Group (NZ)
Photography by Rene Vaile
Additional photography on pages 83 and 99 by Holly Houston
Prepress by Image Centre, Ltd
Printed in China by Leo Paper Products Ltd

ISBN 978 0 14356712 7

A catalogue record for this book is available
from the National Library of New Zealand.

www.penguin.co.nz

Contents

My Story

Baking has been a part of my life for as long as I can remember. When I was two I would sit in on my mother's Home Economics classes at Taupo College. There were no Home Ec. teachers in Taupo at the time so Mum had returned to the classroom, taking me with her – it wasn't so PC in those days! I must have learnt something there, as throughout my life baking has always come easily to me, and over the years it has got me through some tight times.

At art school in Sydney I would bake cookies, cakes and slices at night to sell at the supply store on campus in exchange for art materials. After graduating, I worked at Sweet Art in Sydney sculpting cakes. We produced ocean liners and perfume bottles out of cake and sugar for product launches, and advertising and high-society do's.

Years later, back in New Zealand with two children in tow, I once again began baking at night, creating sculptured cakes for weddings and other special occasions. Eventually I opened Ice It in Devonport – my first serious business venture and a steep learning curve.

After five years of juggling solo parenthood and a business I sold up and moved to Christchurch for a change of pace. Here I met Martin Aspinwall from Canterbury Cheesemongers, who gave me a brief introduction to pastry and English baking. I was hooked. I returned to Auckland without enough capital to open a business so I took my baking to where the people were, selling it at weekend markets. After a couple of years I had built up enough of a following to open a tiny kitchen in the middle of suburbia.

Small Beginnings

My daughter Holly and I and a group of friends got together $3000 and started having fun in the kitchen. We opened Little and Friday in an old butcher's shop, which we intended to use as a catering kitchen to produce food for the markets. The store had a wide plate-glass frontage and before I knew it, people were coming in to buy our brioche straight from the oven.

Initially we would prep all week, bake madly on Thursday night and open the doors to customers on Fridays only. In the morning the counter would be packed with goodies that would sell throughout the day, along with fresh espresso. Gradually, because people could see us working in the kitchen every day and smell the cakes baking, customers began knocking on the door on other days looking for their sweet fix. I couldn't say no – so Little and Friday was no longer so little, or only open on Fridays.

After a year, we were able to expand into the shop next door. This meant we could create a more café-like space, with seating and shelves for retail. Still on a tight budget we trawled TradeMe for cheap furniture, which we painted white. Shelves and tables were knocked together with swap-a-crates, while customers emptied out their cupboards to gift us with mismatching crockery and cutlery.

We had no idea our little venture would become what it is today. We now have two Little and Fridays, both open seven days a week, and 25 staff.

Ethics

From the very beginning, I've wanted to create a positive food business that is largely organic. I abhor factory farming, so we only use free-range meat; produce that has been grown and treated with respect. At first it seemed impossible to accommodate the costs of organic free-range food on a commercial basis, but without realising it we are already halfway there. We have recently invested in raised planter beds out the back of our Belmont store, in which we grow all our own greens, herbs, tomatoes and edible flowers.

We've developed a very close relationship with an organic free-range pig and chicken farmer, who we give our food scraps to in return for free-range eggs and eventually free-range pork. It is so rewarding to be involved in the process of natural farming, and for the business to be closely connected to the food source. It also halves our rubbish waste.

I like to employ people who have a passion for food – not necessarily trained chefs. You can teach baking but you can't teach passion. Most of my staff have never baked before, but love what we are about and love food. When the produce is grown and harvested with respect, it is important for us to treat it with respect and enjoy what we create. The produce needs to be top quality, the staff preparing and selling the food need to feel good, and the end result is happy customers!

Our Recipes

These recipes are the accumulation of a life spent with food. Ideas have stemmed from family, cookbooks and colleagues, and have reworked themselves into what I use in our kitchen today. I am an intuitive baker, not a classically trained one.

I have also learnt from my many mistakes and failures. Someone can teach you how to bake, but I believe one really masters the art by repeatedly baking and getting a feel for the ingredients and processes. This is the key to being a great baker – to instinctively know when a cake batter is too wet, or how the weather is affecting your recipe, and what to do to make it right. I get a lot of pleasure from experimentation, but it is important to have accurate measurements as your starting point. Make sure to have fun when you're cooking,

relish the process of creating something from nothing. It is okay to make mistakes – this is how you learn what works and what doesn't.

A Day in the Life of Little and Friday

Our day in Eversleigh Road starts at 4 a.m. There is little chatter this early: the staff begin preparing the brioches, doughs and pastries for the day. This is my favorite time, watching the sun rise. Early joggers and dog walkers look in longingly as mouth-watering smells waft out of the kitchen while we start pulling trayfuls of tarts and cheese straws out of the hot ovens. By 7.30 the barista is on board, providing the kitchen staff with their much-needed morning shot of caffeine. Our delivery van is loaded with product, ready to head to our Newmarket outlet. Slowly the customers start rolling in, regulars appearing early to get the pick of the day's selection.

Little and Friday has become the bustling neighbourhood local: parents congregate around the communal table to catch up while kids entertain themselves covering the pavement in chalk drawings. By 10 a.m. the sleepy street is overrun with foodies from further afield, who appreciate seeing bakers bringing trays laden with treats straight from the ovens to their plates. Couples perch on beer crates outside, sipping lattes and watching the kitchen team through the plate-glass windows, hard at work icing cakes and filling quiches. As the day goes on, the cabinet and shelves empty out, the ovens are turned off and latecomers scavenge through the slim pickings of the day's leftovers. The street breathes a sigh of relief and reverts back to its former sleepy self – until tomorrow.

Cakes & Loaves

Little and Friday started out as a cake shop, and cakes are my first love. I've developed and used these recipes continuously over the years, so they are all tried and true. A large cake can be adapted into small cakes, and vice versa, so I've given instructions and cooking times for both. We love making the petites – they're great for a high tea.

Lemon & Coconut Cakes

Carrot Cake

Lemon Madeira Loaf

Raspberry & Coconut Friands

Sultana Loaf

Banana Cakes

Orange & Rosewater Cakes

Chocolate Cake

Chocolate Lamingtons

Ginger & Honey Loaf

Eccles Cakes

Baci Cakes

Christmas Cake

Lemon & Coconut Cakes

These Lemon & Coconut Cakes are our most popular by miles. They are also probably the most difficult to make, but well worth the effort.

300g unsalted butter, softened
zest of 2 lemons
2½ cups caster sugar
7 eggs
2½ cups flour, sifted
2½ tsp baking powder
5 cups coconut thread
¾ cup sour cream

Lemon Syrup

1 cup caster sugar
½ cup freshly squeezed lemon juice
2 cups water
2 tbsp lemon zest

To assemble

1 cup Lemon Curd (see page 160)
1 recipe Cream Cheese Icing (see page 158)
Candied Lemon Zest, to decorate (see page 156)

Makes 12 small cakes or one 23cm double-layer cake

1. Preheat oven to 150°C. Grease two 6-hole Texas muffin trays or two 23cm cake tins and line bottoms and sides with baking paper cut to fit exactly.
2. Using an electric mixer, beat butter, lemon zest and sugar on a medium speed until fluffy and light in colour.
3. Add eggs one at a time, mixing well after each addition. Regularly scrape down sides of bowl with a spatula.
4. Sift flour and baking powder over butter mixture and mix on low speed. Be careful not to over-mix.
5. Using a spatula, fold through coconut and sour cream.
6. Divide mixture evenly between prepared cake tins. Bake in centre of oven for 30–35 minutes for small cakes and 55 minutes for large cakes, or until the tops spring back when lightly touched and a skewer comes out clean when inserted into the middle of the cakes.
7. To make Lemon Syrup, place ingredients in a saucepan over a low heat. Stir until sugar is dissolved. Increase heat and boil for 5 minutes or until syrupy.
8. Pour hot syrup over cakes while hot. Let cakes cool completely in their tins on a wire rack before turning out.
9. If making small cakes, carefully cut them in half horizontally. Spread half a cup of Lemon Curd over bottom layers. Spread a thick layer of Cream Cheese Icing over Lemon Curd. Place second cake layer on top. Spread with rest of Cream Cheese Icing, drizzle with extra Lemon Curd and garnish with Candied Lemon Zest and edible flowers.

little and friday.

Kitchen Notes

These cakes will keep for about three days
depending on temperature. It's best to bake them
a day in advance to cool before assembling.

Carrot Cake

Studded with ginger, dates and chocolate,
this Carrot Cake is thoroughly addictive.

Makes one 23cm cake

½ cup walnuts

2 cups flour

2 tsp baking powder

1 tsp ground cinnamon

1 tsp freshly grated nutmeg

1 tsp ground ginger

4 eggs

1 cup oil

1 cup brown sugar

2 cups grated carrot

2 tbsp chopped Candied Orange
Peel (see page 156)

1 tbsp chopped crystallised
ginger

100g good-quality chocolate,
chopped

½ cup chopped dates

To decorate

1 recipe Cream Cheese Icing
(see page 158)

Candied Carrots (see page 157),
to garnish

1. Preheat oven to 160°C. Grease a 23cm cake tin and line the bottom and sides with baking paper cut to fit exactly.
2. Place walnuts on a baking tray and roast for 5 minutes. Set aside.
3. Sift flour, baking powder and spices into a large mixing bowl.
4. In a separate bowl, beat eggs until combined. Add oil and sugar and beat to combine.
5. Add grated carrot, roasted walnuts, Candied Orange Peel, crystallised ginger, chocolate and dates, and combine. Add to the flour mixture and stir to combine.
6. Spoon batter into prepared cake tin and bake for 50–60 minutes or until the top springs back when touched lightly and a skewer comes out clean when inserted into the middle of the cake.
7. Let the cake cool completely in the tin before turning out and peeling off the baking paper.
8. Ice the top with Cream Cheese Icing and garnish with Candied Carrots.

Lemon Madeira Loaf

This is a moreish buttery loaf to have with a cup of tea. If you love a strong, lemony flavour add an extra coat of Lemon Glaze.

350g unsalted butter
1¼ cups caster sugar
6 eggs
zest and juice of 3 lemons
1¼ cups flour
1 tsp baking powder
1 cup ground almonds

Lemon Glaze

2 lemons, juiced
1 cup caster sugar
or icing sugar
1 cup water

Makes 2 loaves

1. Preheat oven to 170°C. Grease two 22cm × 11cm loaf tins and line with baking paper.
2. Using an electric mixer, cream butter and sugar until light and fluffy. Add eggs one at a time, making sure each egg is well combined before adding the next.
3. Add lemon zest and juice and mix to combine.
4. Sift flour and baking powder together and fold through egg mixture with the ground almonds. Do not over-mix.
5. Spoon mixture into loaf tins, filling to 1cm below the rim. Place in the centre of the oven and bake for 55 minutes, turning after 25 minutes. Loaves are ready when the tops bounce back when lightly touched.
6. To make Lemon Glaze, place ingredients in a saucepan. Boil until sugar dissolves.
7. Remove loaves from tins while still hot and using a pastry brush paint tops with hot Lemon Glaze.

Kitchen Notes
For a thicker glaze, use icing sugar instead of caster sugar.

Raspberry &
Coconut Friands

These can be made gluten-free by replacing the flour
with an equivalent measure of rice flour. The generous measure of
raspberries makes for a really fruity, moist friand.

250g unsalted butter

2¾ cups icing sugar

1 cup flour

1 tsp baking powder

1 cup ground almonds

2 cups coconut thread

10 egg whites

pulp from 6 passionfruit
(optional)

6 cups frozen raspberries

icing sugar, to decorate

Makes 12

1. Preheat oven to 180°C. Grease two 6-hole Texas muffin trays
   and line bottoms and sides with baking paper so that the
   paper protrudes 2.5cm above the tin.
2. Melt butter and set aside to cool.
3. Sift icing sugar, flour and baking powder into a bowl. Add
   ground almonds and coconut and stir to combine.
4. Whisk egg whites until soft peaks form. Add egg whites,
   melted butter and passionfruit pulp to dry ingredients and
   fold in until just combined.
5. Half fill prepared tins with mixture, then sprinkle on a
   handful of raspberries. Top with more mixture to just below
   the top of the tin, and sprinkle over more raspberries.
6. Bake for 40 minutes until friands are golden, but still moist
   in the centre when tested with a skewer, and the tops spring
   back when lightly touched.
7. Cool in tin before turning out onto a wire rack. Dust friands
   with sifted icing sugar.

Kitchen Notes

This recipe is just as yummy without the passionfruit. The friands will
keep for three days in an airtight container.

little and friday.

Sultana Loaf

This is one of my mother's recipes from the sixties.

2 cups caster sugar

2 tbsp unsalted butter

2 cups water

500g sultanas

4 cups flour

1 tsp baking soda

1 tsp ground cloves

1 tsp mixed spice

½ tsp salt

1 tbsp Candied Orange Peel
(see page 156), chopped

Makes 2 loaves

1. Preheat oven to 180°C. Grease and line two 22cm × 11cm loaf tins with baking paper.
2. In a large saucepan, combine sugar, butter, water and sultanas and bring to the boil. Turn down heat and simmer for 10 minutes. Remove from heat and allow to cool.
3. Sift flour, baking soda, spices and salt together and using a large spoon fold through sultana mixture. Fold through Candied Orange Peel.
4. Spoon into prepared loaf tins and bake in the centre of the oven for 50 minutes to 1 hour, turning tins after 30 minutes. Loaves are ready when the tops bounce back when lightly touched.

Banana Cakes

This is our interpretation of the *Edmonds Cookbook*
Banana Cake. We make it as a double-layer cake sandwiched
together with gooey caramel and mascarpone.

2 cups flour

1 tsp baking powder

pinch of salt

125g unsalted butter, softened

¾ cup caster sugar

2 eggs

3 cups mashed banana

1 tsp baking soda

4 tbsp hot milk

1 cup walnuts

To assemble

½ cup Caramel (see page 161)

¼ cup mascarpone

1 recipe Cream Cheese Icing
(see page 158)

chopped walnuts or banana
chips, to decorate

Makes 12 small cakes or one 23cm double-layer cake

1. Preheat oven to 160°C. Grease two 6-hole Texas muffin trays
   or two 23cm cake tins and line the bottom and sides with
   baking paper cut to fit exactly.
2. Sift flour, baking powder and salt into a bowl and set aside.
3. Using an electric mixer, beat the butter on a low speed until
   light and creamy.
4. Slowly add sugar and continue to beat on low speed until
   light in colour and fluffy.
5. Add eggs one at a time, mixing well after each addition, and
   making sure to incorporate each egg before adding the next.
   Stop the mixer and scrape down the sides of the bowl with a
   spatula. With the mixer on low speed add the banana.
6. Dissolve baking soda in hot milk.
7. Fold flour mixture and milk into the banana mixture in three
   equal measures. Lastly, fold in walnuts.
8. Divide mixture evenly between prepared cake tins and bake
   for 20–25 minutes for small cakes or 45 minutes for large
   cakes, or until the tops spring back when touched lightly and
   a skewer comes out clean when inserted into the middle.
9. Let cakes cool completely in tins before turning out.
10. If making small cakes, carefully cut them in half horizontally.
    To assemble the cakes, spread Caramel over bottom layer,
    then spread a thin layer of mascarpone over the top. Place
    second cake layer on top. Spread with a thick layer of Cream
    Cheese Icing. Drizzle with extra Caramel and decorate with
    walnuts or banana chips.

little and friday.

Kitchen Notes

Place in an airtight container and store in a cool
place (not the refrigerator) for up to three days.
The banana flavour gets better with age at room
temperature.

Orange & Rosewater Cakes

These moist gluten-free cakes are made with an Orange Slush that needs to be made a day ahead and refrigerated.

Orange Slush

4 oranges

Cake

2 cups ground almonds

1 tsp baking powder

8 eggs

2 cups caster sugar

2 cups Orange Slush

¼ cup rosewater

To decorate

250g mascarpone

Candied Orange Peel
(see page 156)

Makes 6 small cakes or one 23cm cake

1. To make the Orange Slush, wash then chop oranges, skins and all, into 1cm cubes. Place in a heavy-based saucepan and cover with water. Bring to the boil and cook for about 30 minutes or until oranges soften and the water is mostly evaporated. Blend in a food processor until oranges become a thick, smooth slush. Refrigerate overnight.
2. To make the cakes, preheat oven to 180°C. Grease a 6-hole Texas muffin tray or a 23cm cake tin and line the bottom and sides with baking paper. If using muffin tins, the paper should protrude 2.5cm above each hole.
3. Combine ground almonds and baking powder.
4. In a separate bowl, mix eggs and sugar with a hand whisk until sugar is dissolved. Do not over-beat the eggs as this will aerate the mixture.
5. Add Orange Slush and ground almonds to egg mixture and stir gently until well combined.
6. Pour cake mixture into prepared tins and bake for approximately 25 minutes for small cakes or 60 minutes for a large cake, or until the tops spring back when touched lightly and a skewer comes out clean when inserted into the middle of the cakes.
7. While still hot from the oven, pour rosewater over the cakes and leave to cool for 10 minutes before inverting onto a wire rack.
8. Decorate with quenelles of mascarpone and Candied Orange Peel.

little and friday.

Chocolate Cake

This is a delicious, moist chocolate cake which is made with oil so it keeps for days. The sugar syrup adds extra sweetness but can be omitted.

5 eggs
2½ cups caster sugar
300ml canola oil
¼ cup strong black coffee, preferably espresso
1 tsp vanilla essence or paste
250g good-quality chocolate, melted
2 cups flour
2 tsp baking powder
1 cup cocoa
2 tsp ground cinnamon
200ml milk

Sugar Syrup

1 cup caster sugar
2 cups water

To assemble

3½ cups Chocolate Ganache (see page 162)
1 cup Raspberry Coulis (see page 161)
250g mascarpone
½ cup fresh raspberries or edible flowers, to garnish

Makes one 23cm double-layer cake

1. To prepare the cake, preheat oven to 150ºC. Grease two 23cm round tins and line the bottom and sides with baking paper cut to fit exactly.
2. Using an electric mixer, beat eggs and sugar at a medium-high speed until mixture becomes pale, voluminous and falls from the beater in a wide ribbon that holds its form before dissolving back into the mixture.
3. Keep beater on medium speed and slowly drizzle in oil, being careful not to pour too quickly or the mixture will lose volume.
4. Add coffee, vanilla and melted chocolate. Use a spatula to scrape the bottom of the bowl and make sure the chocolate is thoroughly mixed in.
5. Sift flour, baking powder, cocoa and cinnamon into a bowl.
6. Using a large metal spoon, fold a third of the dry ingredients into chocolate mixture. When almost combined, add a third of the milk. Continue in this way until all combined.
7. Pour batter into prepared tins and bake for 45 minutes, or until the tops spring back when touched lightly and a skewer comes out clean when inserted into the middle of the cakes.
8. To make the syrup, place ingredients in a saucepan on a low heat, stirring until sugar is dissolved. Increase heat and boil for 5 minutes or until syrupy.
9. Pour hot syrup over the cakes and cool completely in their tins on a wire rack. When cool, turn out by inverting the tins then turn cakes upright.

little and friday.

10. To assemble, spread ¾ cup Chocolate Ganache over one cake layer. Spread a thin layer of Raspberry Coulis then a thick layer of mascarpone over the Ganache.

11. Place the second cake on top. Spread with remaining Ganache, drizzle with Raspberry Coulis and garnish with raspberries or flowers.

Kitchen Notes

The key to the cake's decadence is using really good-quality dark Dutch cocoa and chocolate with a high cocoa content (at least 50 per cent cocoa), such as Callebaut or Valrhona. To melt chocolate, see Helpful Hints, page 171.

It's best to bake this cake a day in advance to allow it to cool completely before assembling.

Chocolate Lamingtons

As a variation on the typical Kiwi lamington, we use chocolate
cake instead of sponge. We make our lamingtons in cone-shaped tins,
but you can make them whatever shape you like.

1 recipe Chocolate Cake
(see page 26)

6 cups Chocolate Ganache (see
page 162)

4 cups coconut thread

Makes 12

1. Preheat oven to 150°C. Grease 12 cone-shaped tins or
   two 6-hole Texas muffin trays and line bottoms and sides
   with baking paper so paper protrudes 2cm above the tin.
2. Prepare Chocolate Cake mixture by following the
   instructions on page 26 from step 1–6.
3. Pour batter into prepared tins and bake for 25 minutes, or
   until the tops spring back when touched lightly and a skewer
   comes out clean when inserted into the middle of the cakes.
   Allow to cool completely.
4. Using a palette knife, thoroughly coat each side of the
   lamington with a thick layer of semi-soft Ganache.
5. Roll each cake in coconut until evenly covered.

Kitchen Notes

You could also make 2 × 20cm square Chocolate Cakes. Bake cakes for
40 minutes or until the cakes spring back when touched. When cool
cut them into 5cm squares.

Ginger & Honey Loaf

I've adapted this recipe from a Hansell's cookbook from the 1920s. Manuka or a good bush honey are worth the extra expense for the beautiful rich flavour they bring – we buy a Great Barrier Island bush honey from a man at the Takapuna Markets.

115g unsalted butter

½ cup golden syrup

½ cup good-quality honey

1 cup brown sugar

2½ cups flour

2½ tsp baking powder

2 tsp ground ginger

1 tsp mixed spice

½ a nutmeg, grated

1 cup milk

1 egg, beaten

Ginger Syrup

1 recipe Sugar Syrup (see page 26)

½ cup ginger syrup (available from specialty stores)

Makes 2 loaves

1. Preheat oven to 180°C. Grease two 22cm × 11cm loaf tins and line with baking paper.
2. In a saucepan, combine butter, golden syrup, honey and sugar, and heat gently, stirring with a wooden spoon until combined and mixture is hot. Remove from heat.
3. Sift dry ingredients into a bowl. Make a well in the centre and pour butter mixture into dry ingredients. Stir to combine, then add milk and egg. The mixture will be quite runny.
4. Pour into loaf tins. Bake for 60 minutes. Loaves are ready when the tops spring back when lightly touched and a skewer comes out clean when inserted into the middle of the loaf.
5. While the loaf is cooking, prepare the Ginger Syrup. Place Sugar Syrup in a saucepan on a low heat and when hot add ginger syrup, stirring until fully combined and right consistency is reached.
6. Remove loaves from oven and pour ½ cup Ginger Syrup over each while still in the tins. Remove from tins when cool.

Kitchen Notes

Ginger syrup can also be used for hot drinks and cocktails. We use Hakanoa organic syrup but there are a variety of brands available.

Eccles Cakes

The eccles cake is an old-fashioned English pastry best served with a fresh brew of English Breakfast tea and traditionally accompanied by a good strong cheese.

220g unsalted butter

3½ cups currants

1 whole nutmeg, grated

2 tsp ground cinnamon

¼ cup chopped Candied Orange Peel (see page 156)

5 tbsp boiling water

1 sheet Flaky Pastry (see page 116)

Egg Wash (see page 117)

demerara sugar, for topping

Makes 6

1. Melt butter over a medium heat until golden.
2. Mix currants, spices and Candied Orange Peel together in a bowl. Pour over boiling water and soak for 5 minutes.
3. Add melted butter and stir until currants are coated. Leave to sit for 20 minutes.
4. Preheat oven to 200°C. On a floured bench, roll pastry out to 3mm thick and cut into six 12cm squares.
5. Spoon fruit mixture evenly into the centre of each pastry square and brush edges of pastry sparingly with Egg Wash.
6. Bring pastry corners together and squeeze to seal. Use scissors to cut off any excess pastry.
7. Turn cakes smooth side up, glaze with Egg Wash and sprinkle generously with demerara sugar. Using scissors or a knife, cut three slits in the centre of the cakes.
8. Bake for approximately 20–25 minutes or until golden. Best eaten on the same day.

Baci Cakes

Our gluten-free Baci Cakes are gleaned from a recipe from Phillippa Grogan, who owns a bakery in Melbourne. They take a bit of patience and gentle hands, but the result is hugely popular.

285g good-quality dark chocolate

1¼ cups caster sugar

225g unsalted butter, softened

7 eggs, separated

2 cups finely ground hazelnuts (see Kitchen Notes)

¼ cup strong black coffee, preferably espresso

To assemble

3 cups Chocolate Ganache (see page 162)

1–2 cups finely ground hazelnuts

12 Chocolate Spirals (see page 162), to garnish

Makes 12

1. To prepare the cakes, preheat oven to 170°C. Grease two 6-hole Texas muffin trays with cooking spray and line bottoms and sides with baking paper so paper protrudes 2cm above the tin.
2. Melt chocolate over a bowl of simmering water. Remove from heat and cool.
3. Using an electric mixer, beat sugar and butter until light and fluffy. Add egg yolks one at a time, beating well after each addition.
4. Add cooled chocolate and combine well with a metal spoon. Fold in hazelnuts and coffee.
5. Using an electric mixer, whisk egg whites until soft peaks form.
6. Fold a third of the egg whites into chocolate mixture to loosen using a metal spoon, then fold in remaining egg whites until just combined.
7. Spoon mixture into prepared tins, filling to just below the top.
8. Bake for 25 minutes until just cooked. Cakes should form an outer crust, but still be a little moist in the centre when tested with a skewer.
9. Leave cakes in tins to cool for 10 minutes before inverting onto a wire rack.
10. To assemble the cakes, use a palette knife to cover the outside of each cake with softened Chocolate Ganache. Roll in ground hazelnuts so sides are coated. Garnish with a dollop of firm Ganache and top with a Chocolate Spiral.

little and friday.

Kitchen Notes

To soften Chocolate Ganache, place in a metal bowl over a saucepan of simmering water and stir until a spreadable consistency. Alternatively, use a microwave.

Roast hazelnuts in a 180°C oven for 5–10 minutes. Cool and rub to remove skins before grinding finely in a food processor. Alternatively, use ground almonds.

Christmas Cake

Bake the cake weeks in advance to alleviate the stresses of Christmas
and pour over brandy every fortnight until you are ready to ice it.

Fruit Mix

1 cup each sultanas, currants, raisins
½ cup each diced prunes, dates, figs, mixed peel
2 tbsp marmalade
1 tbsp lemon zest
1 tbsp orange zest
1 apple, peeled and grated
½ cup brandy

Cake

100g unsalted butter
¾ cup brown sugar
3 eggs
1 cup flour
2 tbsp cocoa
1 tsp ground cinnamon
1 tsp mixed spice
½ tsp salt
75g dark chocolate, chopped

Marzipan

2 cups ground almonds
½ cup caster sugar
½ cup icing sugar
1 egg
1 tsp orange blossom water

Makes 1 cake

1. To prepare fruit mix, combine fruit in a large bowl and pour over half the brandy. Allow fruit to soak up brandy overnight and pour over remaining brandy. Stir daily for up to 3 weeks before making cake.

2. To prepare cake, preheat oven to 140°C. Grease a 20cm square tin and line with a double layer of baking paper. Wrap a double layer of newspaper around sides of tin and secure with string to prevent edges of cake browning too quickly.

3. Using an electric mixer, cream butter and sugar. Add eggs one at a time, beating well after each addition.

4. Using a spatula, fold through sifted flour, cocoa, spices and salt. Fold through chopped chocolate and fruit mix.

5. Bake for 3 hours. Cool completely before removing from tin. Store cake in an airtight container until ready to ice.

6. To make Marzipan, combine all ingredients in a large bowl. Turn out onto a floured bench and lightly knead. Roll out to 1cm thick between two layers of baking paper. This will prevent Marzipan sticking to rolling pin.

7. Lay Marzipan over cake and cut to size. Decorate with dried fruit and nuts. We use dried pears, cranberries, pistachios, walnuts and star anise. For a really special cake, you can lay gold leaf over the star anise. We decorate our cakes just before Christmas, but it can be done up to 2 weeks prior to serving.

little and friday.

Biscuits, Slices & Sweets

All of these recipes keep well and stored properly will last for up to three weeks – if they don't get eaten sooner. We recommend making extra batches to give to family and friends for special occasions, and at Little and Friday customers frequently buy our goodies to take along to dinner parties in place of a bottle of wine.

Caramel Slice

A true classic, we can never keep up with the demand for this slice.

Base
175g unsalted butter, softened
2 cups icing sugar
½ tsp vanilla essence or paste
1 egg
½ cup Dutch cocoa
1½ cups flour
½ tsp salt

Caramel
2 × 395g tins sweetened condensed milk
200ml golden syrup
100g unsalted butter
1 cup roasted hazelnuts, chopped

Topping
¾ cup Chocolate Ganache (see page 162)

Makes approx. 24 slices

1. Preheat oven to 150°C. Grease a 25cm square tin and line the bottom and sides with baking paper.
2. Using an electric mixer, cream butter, icing sugar and vanilla until light and fluffy. Add egg and beat until well combined. Sift cocoa, flour and salt together then mix thoroughly into the butter mixture.
3. Press mixture firmly into base of prepared tin. Bake for 10–15 minutes in centre of oven.
4. While base is cooking, prepare Caramel. Combine all ingredients in a saucepan and melt slowly over a low heat. Pour over cooked base.
5. Return to oven for a further 15 minutes or until set.
6. When cool, spread a thin layer of hot Chocolate Ganache over Caramel. When Ganache has set, place in refrigerator until firm. Slice using a very sharp knife dipped in boiling water. Store in refrigerator.

Pistachio Shortbread Crescents

I have been making these biscuits for years and have adapted the recipe at times for a change. You can replace the pistachios with walnuts and use lemon rind in place of the orange.

250g unsalted butter
1 cup caster sugar
2 egg yolks
6 tbsp orange juice
4 cups flour
1½ tsp baking powder
1 cup pistachios, shelled
1 tsp crushed cardamom seeds
⅓ cup rosewater
icing sugar, to decorate

Makes approx. 20

1. Preheat oven to 180°C. Line two baking trays with baking paper.
2. Cream butter and sugar with an electric mixer until light and fluffy. Stop and scrape down sides of bowl frequently to ensure all ingredients are thoroughly combined.
3. Add egg yolks one at a time and beat well. Ensure each yolk is integrated before adding the next. Beat in orange juice.
4. In a separate bowl, combine flour, baking powder, pistachios and cardamom. Gently fold into butter mixture, being careful not to overwork the dough.
5. Using a tablespoon, roll spoonfuls of cookie mixture into balls and place at least 3cm apart on lined baking trays. Mould each ball into a crescent shape.
6. Bake for 15-20 minutes. Biscuits are ready when they slide freely on the paper when the tray is tipped.
7. Using a pastry brush, paint hot biscuits with rosewater and dust liberally with sifted icing sugar.

Biscotti

These last for weeks and are really good dunked
into a strong coffee.

4 cups flour
3 tsp baking powder
1½ cups brown sugar
2 tsp vanilla essence or paste
2 cups cranberries
2 cups pistachios
zest of 1 orange
4 eggs

Makes approx. 40

1. Preheat oven to 180°C. Line two baking trays with baking paper.
2. Sift flour and baking powder into a large bowl.
3. Stir in remaining ingredients, except eggs.
4. Beat eggs separately and add to dry ingredients. Using a wooden spoon, mix until combined. (The mixture will be quite dry and crumbly.)
5. Using your hands, work the mixture together and shape into two logs measuring approximately 20cm. Place on lined tray and bake for 30 minutes.
6. Remove from oven and slice each log with a serrated knife into approximately 20 1cm-wide slices. The slices should be slightly moist in the centre.
7. Reduce oven to 140°C. Lay cut slices on lined baking trays and return to oven for 20 minutes, until they are dry and hard. Store in an airtight container for up to 4 weeks.

Kitchen Notes

We like to dip one edge of our cooked biscotti in melted white or dark chocolate.

As a variation to this biscotti mix, we also make Coffee & Walnut Biscotti by substituting the cranberries, pistachios and orange zest with 4 cups walnuts and 1 tbsp ground instant coffee. Another variation is Chocolate & Hazelnut Biscotti, which are made by replacing the cranberries, pistachios and orange zest with 4 cups hazelnuts and ½ cup cocoa. Also add an extra egg in this recipe.

little and friday.

Shortbread

This recipe is from Claire Clarke, the pastry chef at the French Laundry in California. A simple recipe from her mother, it creates a really short, lovely biscuit.

1½ cups flour

⅓ cup caster sugar

seeds from 1 vanilla pod or
½ tsp vanilla essence or paste

150g unsalted butter, at room temperature

extra caster sugar, for dusting

Makes 15 bars

1. Preheat oven to 180°C. Line a baking tray with baking paper.
2. Sift flour into a bowl and mix in sugar and vanilla.
3. Rub butter into dry ingredients with your fingertips until mixture resembles coarse breadcrumbs.
4. Using your hands, work the mixture together to form a ball. Place between two sheets of baking paper. This prevents rolling pin sticking to dough. It also gives a nice smooth finish.
5. Roll dough out to 2cm thick and cut into 15 even-sized rectangles. Place shortbread at least 3cm apart on lined baking tray.
6. Bake for 15 minutes or until slightly golden. Remove from oven and dust liberally with caster sugar.

Anzac Biscuits

A classic Kiwi recipe made and eaten by millions of
home cooks over the years.

1 cup flour

1 cup coconut thread

⅔ cup tightly packed brown
sugar

1 cup jumbo rolled oats

125g unsalted butter

2 tbsp golden syrup

½ tsp baking soda

2 tbsp boiling water

200g good-quality dark
chocolate, melted (optional)

Makes approx. 20

1. Preheat oven to 160°C. Line two baking trays with baking
   paper.
2. Place flour, coconut, sugar and oats into a mixing bowl and
   combine.
3. Melt butter and golden syrup in a saucepan over a medium
   heat. While this is melting, place baking soda in a bowl, add
   boiling water and stir. As it fluffs up, stir into butter mixture.
4. Quickly pour butter mixture over dry ingredients while still
   fluffy. Stir to combine.
5. Using a tablespoon, roll spoonfuls of mixture into balls and
   place 3cm apart on prepared trays, flattening them slightly.
   Bake for 15-20 minutes or until biscuits are golden.
6. Once cool, dip edges of biscuits in melted chocolate, if
   desired.

Cranberry Macaroons

This is a modern take on a 1950s recipe I found in one
of my mother's Home Ec. manuals. You don't need to beat the
egg whites, and the key to success is being very vigilant
when heating the egg mixture.

3 egg whites
1¼ cups caster sugar
1 tbsp liquid glucose
½ tsp vanilla essence or paste
¼ cup very finely chopped
cranberries
3 cups coconut thread
¾ cup flour, sifted

Makes 24

1. Line two baking trays with baking paper.
2. Place egg whites, sugar, liquid glucose and vanilla essence
   in a bowl in a sink of hot water (or a double boiler over a
   low heat) and combine very gently, stirring with a whisk,
   until mixture is just warm and sugar crystals have melted.
   Be careful not to cook the egg whites – the mixture should
   remain clear in colour. Remove from heat.
3. Using a large metal spoon, fold in remaining ingredients,
   taking care not to over-mix.
4. Place teaspoonfuls of mixture onto the lined trays, 5cm
   apart to allow for spread, then leave at room temperature for
   several hours to dry out. Once a dry skin has formed over
   the surface of the macaroons they are ready to cook.
5. Preheat oven to 150°C. Bake for 15–20 minutes until
   macaroons are a light golden colour. Allow to cool before
   removing from baking paper.

Kitchen Notes

We like to dot the tops of the Macaroons with whole cranberries.

If it is a wet day drying out the mixture may be difficult. You could try
placing trays in the hot water cupboard or turning on a dehumidifier.

Try changing out the cranberries for glacé cherries – very 1950s!

little and friday.

Chocolate Chip Cookies

Sometimes we use a combination of milk, white and dark chocolate to make these scrumptious cookies. The chunkier the chocolate, the better.

125g unsalted butter, at room temperature

1¼ cups tightly packed brown sugar

1 tsp vanilla essence or paste

1 egg, lightly beaten

1½ cups flour

½ tsp baking powder

pinch of salt

250g good-quality chocolate, roughly chopped

Makes approx. 20

1. Preheat oven to 180°C. Line a baking tray with baking paper.
2. Place butter and sugar in a bowl and beat with an electric mixer until light and creamy. Scrape down sides to ensure all ingredients are thoroughly mixed.
3. Add vanilla and egg to butter mixture and beat again.
4. Sift flour, baking powder and salt over butter mixture and, using a wooden spoon, stir until just combined. Fold through chopped chocolate.
5. Using a tablespoon, roll spoonfuls of cookie mixture into balls and place 3cm apart on lined baking trays, flattening slightly with a fork. Bake for 15-20 minutes until pale golden.

little and friday.

eversleigh road, takapuna   phone: four nine nine eight five two seven

Lemon Coconut Slice

This delicious recipe was given to me by Katie, a really
gifted baker I was lucky enough to have help me out
during a brief venture in Christchurch.

Base

175g unsalted butter, softened
1½ cups icing sugar
½ tsp vanilla essence or paste
1 egg
2 cups desiccated coconut
1½ cups flour

Filling

2 × 395g tins sweetened
condensed milk
250ml lemon juice
200ml passionfruit pulp
8 egg yolks

Meringue

8 egg whites
½ cup caster sugar
2 cups coconut thread
½ tsp salt
½ tsp vanilla essence or paste

Makes approx. 24 slices

1. Preheat oven to 150°C. Grease a 25cm square tin and line the
   bottom and sides with baking paper.
2. To prepare base, cream butter, icing sugar and vanilla with
   an electric mixer until light and fluffy. Add egg and beat until
   well combined.
3. Using a wooden spoon, fold through coconut and flour until
   combined.
4. Press mixture firmly into prepared tin. Bake for 10 minutes
   in centre of oven.
5. While base is cooking, prepare filling. Combine all ingredients
   in a bowl. Pour over cooked base and return to oven for a
   further 15 minutes until set.
6. Prepare meringue by whisking egg whites with an electric
   mixer until soft peaks form. Whisk in sugar, coconut, salt
   and vanilla.
7. Spread meringue evenly over cooked filling. Bake for
   10 minutes or until meringue is light brown. Place in
   refrigerator to set.

Kitchen Notes

When beating egg whites, use eggs at room temperature and a clean, dry bowl. Otherwise the whites will not whip up properly.

Florentines

These are great packaged as a gift at Christmas time.
They will last for weeks.

1 cup flaked almonds

⅓ cup hazelnuts

⅓ cup slivered almonds

⅓ cup pistachios

⅓ cup macadamias

65g unsalted butter

½ cup caster sugar

125ml cream

2 tbsp honey

10 pieces Candied Orange Peel
(see page 156), chopped

300g good-quality dark
chocolate, melted

Makes 24

1. Preheat oven to 170°C. Line bottoms of two 12-hole muffin trays with baking paper.
2. Combine nuts on a lined baking tray and roast until golden, about 10 minutes.
3. Place butter, sugar, cream and honey in a heavy-based saucepan and stir over low heat until dissolved.
4. Turn heat to high. When candy thermometer reaches 118°C remove from heat.
5. Add nuts and Candied Orange Peel to sugar mixture while still hot and stir until all nuts are coated.
6. Spoon mixture into lined muffin trays and press down into tin with the base of a glass to flatten.
7. Bake for 20 minutes until golden. Remove from oven and cool. Florentines should come out of tins easily once cold – simply lever out with a knife.
8. Dip back of each biscuit in melted chocolate.

Kitchen Notes

For best results you will need a candy thermometer. If you don't have one, cook sugar mixture to the 'soft ball' stage. Scoop out a small amount of the sugar mixture with a teaspoon and drop into a glass of cold water. If it retains its shape but is still soft to the touch, the mixture is ready to be removed from the heat.

little and friday.

Raspberry & Chocolate Meringues

These meringues are crisp on the outside with a lovely gooey filling. If freeze-dried raspberries are unavailable, whole pistachio nuts with chocolate is a divine combination.

9 egg whites

2¼ cups caster sugar

½ cup freeze-dried raspberries

½ cup Callebaut chocolate callets or chips

1 cup Raspberry Coulis (see page 161), to serve

whipped cream, to serve

Makes 10 large meringues

1. Preheat oven to 100°C. Line two baking trays with baking paper.
2. Put egg whites and caster sugar in a stainless steel bowl, and place bowl in a sink of hot water. Whisk with a hand whisk until sugar dissolves.
3. Remove bowl from water. Using an electric beater, whisk egg white mixture for 6 minutes until firm peaks form.
4. Gently fold through raspberries and chocolate.
5. Scoop spoonfuls of mixture and drop onto lined baking trays at least 5cm apart.
6. Bake for 1 hour. Turn off oven and do not open door. Leave meringues in oven for at least 1 hour, or overnight, to dry out.
7. Serve with Raspberry Coulis and whipped cream.

Kitchen Notes
Freeze-dried raspberries and Callebaut chocolate are available from specialty food stores. You can also vary the recipe by flavouring the meringue mixture – try folding through 1 cup Caramel (see page 161) or Chocolate Ganache (see page 162).

Panforte

I love the white chocolate version of this recipe.
It is always good around Christmastime.

3 cups roughly chopped good-quality white chocolate

1 cup liquid glucose

1 cup manuka honey

3 cups flour

2 cups dried figs, chopped

3 cups walnut halves

Makes approx. 60 squares

1. Preheat oven to 160°C. Line base and sides of a 25cm square tin with baking paper.
2. Place chopped chocolate in freezer for at least 10 minutes.
3. Put glucose and honey in a heavy-based saucepan and cook over a medium heat until honey has dissolved. Bring to the boil. Simmer for 2 minutes, remove from heat and allow to cool slightly.
4. In a bowl, mix together flour, figs and walnuts and add to sugar syrup. Add chilled chocolate and stir to combine.
5. Press panforte mixture into base of tin. Bake for 45 minutes or until it bounces back when lightly touched. Allow to cool before cutting into 3cm squares or alternatively into lengths. Store in an airtight container at room temperature for up to 4 weeks.

Kitchen Notes

The white chocolate version of this recipe is our most popular panforte and very versatile. We also make a dark chocolate variation, replacing the white chocolate with dark chocolate (at least 50 per cent cocoa) and the walnuts with roasted hazelnuts. To this mixture we also sometimes add ½ cup good-quality Dutch cocoa to make it extra rich.

Peanut Brittle

Be warned, Peanut Brittle is absolutely addictive! Many of my customers have bought packets, only to return the same day to buy more.

1½ cups caster sugar
½ cup water
⅓ cup liquid glucose
2½ cups blanched peanuts
1 tbsp unsalted butter
½ tsp vanilla essence or paste
½ tsp baking soda

Makes approx. 20 pieces

1. Line a baking tray with baking paper.
2. In a heavy-based saucepan, combine sugar, water and glucose and place over a low heat. Lightly stir with a wooden spoon until sugar just melts.
3. Bring to the boil and cook without stirring until mixture reaches 128°C on a candy thermometer, about 5–8 minutes.
4. Add peanuts and quickly stir once to distribute. Leave on the heat until temperature reaches 154°C on the thermometer.
5. Remove from heat. Quickly stir in butter and vanilla, then baking soda.
6. Quickly pour mixture onto prepared baking tray, spreading it with the back of a spatula or metal spoon to form a 1cm-thick layer.
7. Let the Brittle cool completely before turning it out and breaking into shards. Brittle will keep in an airtight container for up to two weeks.

Kitchen Notes

Try not to stir the mixture too much or it may crystallise.

You'll need to invest in a candy thermometer for best results.

Do not attempt to make this on a rainy day or in humid weather. It will not set!

Liquid glucose is available from specialty food stores.

Chocolate Fudge

Of all our recipes, this is the hardest to get right. I have found it is never successful if I am attempting to multi-task and I would not attempt it on a wet day. I have been making this fudge for over 10 years and am still totally addicted. It's best not to think about your calorie intake when indulging in this treat.

5 cups caster sugar

1 litre cream

2 cups Callebaut chocolate callets or chips or chopped good-quality chocolate (at least 50 per cent cocoa)

60g unsalted butter

1 tbsp liquid glucose

¾ cup Dutch cocoa

Makes approx. 30 squares

1. Grease and line a 20cm × 30cm tin with baking paper. Place all ingredients into a heavy-based saucepan over a high heat. Stir until well combined, but do not beat.

2. Bring to the boil and reduce heat. It is important not to stir the mixture during this period, as sugar will crystallise.

3. If you have a candy thermometer, bring the mixture to 114°C. Otherwise use the soft ball method (see page 58). Again, it is important not to stir during this stage.

4. Remove from heat and, using an electric beater, beat until the mixture thickens to ribbon stage. To test this, turn off the electric beater and raise it from the mixture. The mixture should fall from the beaters and form a ribbon-like pattern that sinks after a few seconds. Do not over-beat it or the sugar will crystallise, making the fudge grainy.

5. Pour mixture into prepared tin. Allow to set overnight at room temperature. Once set, cut into 2cm squares with a sharp knife. Do not store in the refrigerator. This mixture uses fresh cream, so it keeps for 2–3 weeks only in an airtight container before drying out.

Little and Friday's fudge flavours, pictured from top: Raspberry; Lime and Pistachio; Chocolate; Coffee and Walnut; Russian.

little and friday.

Sweet Tarts

Each of these tarts is made with a basic Sweet Pastry recipe. Most can be adapted to make small or large tarts, making them perfect to serve for afternoon tea or as a dessert.

Sweet Pastry

Over the years I have found this pastry to be really easy to handle and it bakes up extremely short, meaning it has a high ratio of butter to flour. It holds its shape and, if rested, doesn't shrink. It also bakes off rather crisp, which is what you want.

2¾ cups flour
1 cup icing sugar
pinch of salt
250g unsalted butter, chopped
1 egg
1 tsp lemon juice
½ tsp lemon zest
vanilla essence or paste, to taste

Makes one 28cm round tart or six 6cm tarts

1. In a food processor, combine flour, icing sugar and salt and pulse in 2-second bursts to aerate and combine.
2. Add butter and pulse until mixture resembles light breadcrumbs.
3. Add egg, lemon juice, zest and vanilla and pulse 10 times. The mixture should look dry and crumbly.
4. Turn out onto a clean work surface and gather mixture together.
5. Gently shape mixture into a ball. Wrap in cling film and refrigerate for 2 hours before using.

Kitchen Notes

This pastry keeps well in the refrigerator for up to two weeks. We often line our tins and freeze them. They can be taken from the freezer and baked immediately. Do not thaw.

Blind baking is the process of baking a tart crust before it is filled. It is necessary when a filling has a shorter bake time than the pastry. Blind baking also helps to prevent pastry becoming soggy from the filling. Line the uncooked pastry with a sheet of baking paper, or use paper patty cases for small tarts, and fill with uncooked rice or dried beans as a weight. Bake the pastry for the required time, then remove the paper and rice before filling.

little and friday.

Citron Tart

Although this recipe has a lot of steps, the end result is well worth the preparation! The citron filling needs to be prepared the day before and you need to allow time to chill the pastry.

1 recipe Sweet Pastry (see page 70)

Candied Lemon Zest (see page 156), to decorate (optional)

Citron Filling

7 eggs

1½ cups caster sugar

240ml cream

zest and juice of 3 large lemons or 6 limes

Makes one 28cm round tart or six 6cm tarts

1. To prepare filling, in a large bowl stir eggs and caster sugar together until sugar is dissolved. Be careful not to aerate the mixture or it will be foamy.

2. Add cream and stir until combined. Add zest and juice and stir another 2 minutes to combine. Once the juice is added, the mixture will appear to separate. Don't worry. Keep stirring until it reaches a smooth, pourable consistency.

3. Pour filling into an airtight container and refrigerate overnight to allow the flavour of the zest to infuse. Return to room temperature before baking.

4. Preheat oven to 180°C. Roll out pastry to 3mm thick, and line a 28cm or six 6cm loose-bottom tart tins, trimming pastry to form a neat edge. Rest pastry case in refrigerator or freezer for at least 30 minutes.

5. Place pastry-lined tart tin on an oven tray. Line pastry case with baking paper, fill with dried beans or uncooked rice and blind bake for 15 minutes.

6. Remove baking paper and beans from pastry case, lower oven to 150°C and bake a further 10 minutes. Allow pastry to cool completely before filling.

7. Reduce oven temperature to 130°C. Stir filling then strain through a sieve to remove zest. Skim any froth from the top.

8. Carefully pour citron filling into prepared pastry case to 3mm below the rim. Scoop off any bubbles with a spoon before baking for 40–50 minutes for a large tart or about 20 minutes for small tarts. Be careful not to overcook, as the

little and friday.

filling will curdle. The cooked filling should be set but will wobble slightly in the centre when the tray is moved.

9. Leave to cool on a wire rack before carefully removing from tin. Decorate with a little Candied Lemon Zest in the centre of the tart.

Fresh Summer Berry Tarts

These are visually stunning. We use whatever berry fruit is available in the hot months. In late summer figs also look pretty.

1 recipe Sweet Pastry (see page 70)

Filling

½ cup Frangipane (see page 158)

1 cup Crème Pâtissière (see page 159)

½ cup Crème Diplomat (see page 159)

6 cups fresh summer berries (raspberries, blackberries, strawberries [halved] and blueberries)

edible flowers (e.g. borage), to garnish

Makes six 6cm tarts or one 12cm × 35cm tart

1. On a lightly floured bench, roll out pastry to 3mm thick and line six 6cm, or a 12cm × 35cm, loose-bottom tart tins, trimming pastry to form a neat edge. Rest pastry cases in refrigerator or freezer for at least 30 minutes.
2. Preheat oven to 180°C. Place tray in oven to heat.
3. Spread 1 tbsp Frangipane over each pastry case. Spoon over 2 tbsp Crème Pâtissière to fill. Top each tart with a small handful of berries.
4. Bake for 20 minutes for small tarts or 40 minutes for a large tart, or until pastry is golden. Leave to cool before removing tarts from tins.
5. Once cool, put a dollop of Crème Diplomat on top of each tart. Arrange fresh berries over tarts and garnish with edible flowers.

little and friday.

Pear Tarts

These tarts are a favourite of mine. They look amazing and are incredibly moreish. They are best served with a big dollop of mascarpone.

1 recipe Sweet Pastry (see page 70)

1 cup Frangipane (see page 158)

6 Poached Pears (see page 164)

1 tbsp manuka honey, to glaze

mascarpone, to serve

Makes six 6cm tarts

1. On a lightly floured bench, roll out pastry to 3mm thick and line six 6cm loose-bottom tart tins. Rest pastry cases in refrigerator or freezer for at least 30 minutes. Place on a baking tray.
2. Preheat oven to 180°C.
3. Spoon 3 tbsp Frangipane into each tart case.
4. Using a sharp paring knife, carefully slice the bottom off each Poached Pear so they sit flat. Keeping the tops intact, cut vertical slices from the stalk of each pear, making each slice a few millimetres apart.
5. Gently spread the pear slices apart to form a circular fan from the stalk. Place a pear fan on top of each tart, twisting slightly so the slices extend to the edges.
6. Bake for 30 minutes or until Frangipane is cooked.
7. Make a honey glaze by melting manuka honey with a dash of boiling water. Using a pastry brush, paint glaze over pears while hot. Leave tarts to cool before removing from tins.

little and friday.

Baked Chocolate Tart

This rich tart calls for really good-quality chocolate.
We use chocolate that is 53 per cent cocoa solids.

1 recipe Sweet Pastry (see page 70)

Filling

3 cups good-quality dark chocolate, chopped

300g unsalted butter, chopped

3 eggs

2 egg yolks

½ cup caster sugar

Makes one 28cm round tart

1. On a lightly floured bench, roll out pastry to 3mm thick, and line a 28cm loose-bottom tart tin, trimming pastry to form a neat edge. Rest pastry case in refrigerator or freezer for at least 30 minutes.
2. Preheat oven to 180°C.
3. Place pastry-lined tart tin on an oven tray. Line pastry case with baking paper, fill with dried beans or uncooked rice, and blind bake for 15 minutes.
4. Remove baking paper and beans from pastry case, lower oven to 150°C and bake a further 10 minutes. Remove pastry case from oven and allow to cool completely before filling. Raise oven temperature to 160°C.
5. To prepare filling, place chocolate and butter in a metal bowl over a saucepan of simmering water. Make sure the bottom is not touching the water, as this will scald the chocolate. Stir with a wooden spoon until melted, then remove from the heat.
6. Place eggs, egg yolks and sugar in a second metal bowl and place over the saucepan of simmering water, ensuring the bowl does not touch the water. Whisk continuously until mixture thickens and sugar is dissolved, approximately 5 minutes. Don't stop whisking or the eggs may begin to cook.
7. Once egg mixture has doubled in volume, remove from the heat. Slowly pour one third of chocolate mixture into thickened eggs, and gently fold. Be careful not to over-mix.
8. When just combined, fold in remaining chocolate mixture and pour into cooked pastry case.

little and friday.

9. Place tart in oven for 10 minutes to cook before removing from oven to cool at room temperature. The mixture will still be wobbly when removed from oven but will set as it cools.

10. When cool, store in refrigerator for up to 3 days. Serve cold.

Rhubarb Tarts

The sweet, sharp flavour of poached rhubarb and berries teamed
with a creamy filling and crisp pastry – a heavenly trio.

1 recipe Sweet Pastry (see page 70)

⅓ cup Frangipane (see page 158)

2 cups Crème Pâtissière (see page 159)

1½ cups frozen or fresh raspberries

5 stalks Poached Rhubarb (see page 164)

icing sugar, sifted, to decorate

Makes six 6cm tarts

1. On a lightly floured bench, roll out pastry to 3mm thick and line six 6cm loose-bottomed tart tins, trimming pastry to form a neat edge. Place lined tins in refrigerator for at least 60 minutes to rest.
2. Preheat oven to 180°C. Place a tray in oven to heat.
3. Spread 1 tbsp Frangipane in each pastry case, and fill to just below rim with Crème Pâtissière.
4. Sprinkle a generous handful of raspberries over the top.
5. Place on heated tray in bottom of oven and bake for 30–35 minutes or until pastry is golden.
6. Remove from oven and top with poached rhubarb. Return to oven and bake a further 10 minutes.
7. Cool and sprinkle with icing sugar. Best eaten the same day.

Kitchen Notes

At Little and Friday we remove the bases from the tart tins before lining with baking paper and pastry, as the pastry sits on a hot tray in the oven. The heat penetrates the pastry and makes it crisper.

Summer Fruit Tarts

We bake with the seasons and therefore love summer for all the
fruit options! We usually use one type of stone fruit per tart,
but feel free to use a combination of all three if you prefer.

1 recipe Sweet Pastry (see
page 70)

mascarpone, to serve (optional)

Filling

½ cup Frangipane (see
page 158)

1 cup Crème Pâtissière (see
page 159)

2 cups frozen or fresh
blackberries (if using nectarines
or apricots, use raspberries
instead)

15 plums, nectarines or
apricots, sliced into wedges

Glaze

2 tbsp manuka honey

2 tsp orange blossom water

Makes six 6cm tarts

1. On a lightly floured bench, roll out pastry to 3mm thick
   and line tart tins, trimming pastry to form a neat edge.
   Rest pastry cases in refrigerator or freezer for at least
   30 minutes.
2. Preheat oven to 180°C. Place tray in oven to heat.
3. Spread 2 tbsp Frangipane over each pastry case. Fill cases
   with Crème Pâtissière to just below rim.
4. Scatter over blackberries or raspberries. Arrange slices of
   stone fruit on top of berries in a spiral, starting from the
   outside edge and working in.
5. Place on tray in oven and bake for 30–35 minutes or until
   pastry is golden. Leave to cool before removing from tin.
6. To prepare glaze, combine manuka honey and orange
   blossom water with a dash of boiling water and brush over
   fruit with a pastry brush while hot. Serve with mascarpone,
   if desired.

Kitchen Notes

At Little and Friday we marinate the sliced stone fruit for 1–2 hours in the juice of 6 oranges, ½ cup caster sugar and 1 tbsp orange blossom water. For an alcoholic alternative, use 1 tbsp Cointreau in place of orange blossom water.

Because tart cases are not blind-baked, placing them onto a preheated tray will ensure they cook quickly and crisp up.

sweet tarts

Walnut & Caramel Tarts

A perfect combination of sweet caramel and nutty walnuts,
these little tarts satisfy any sugar craving.

1 recipe Sweet Pastry (see page 70)

¾ cup Frangipane (see page 158)

1½ cups Caramel (see page 161)

4 cups walnut halves or macadamia nuts

125g good-quality dark chocolate (optional)

Makes 12 small tarts

1. On a lightly floured bench, roll out pastry to 3mm thick and, using a 10cm cookie cutter, or a glass or lid, cut out 12 circles. Use pastry circles to line a 12-hole muffin tray, trimming any overhanging pastry to form a neat edge.
2. Rest uncooked pastry cases in refrigerator or freezer for at least 30 minutes before placing on an oven tray.
3. Preheat oven to 180°C.
4. Fill each case with 1 tbsp Frangipane and bake for 15–20 minutes. Frangipane is cooked when you press it with your finger and it bounces back.
5. Remove from oven and allow to cool before removing pastry shells from tins.
6. Pour Caramel over Frangipane, filling to the rim of the tart. Pile nuts on top and pour over more Caramel. For an added indulgence, dark chocolate can be melted and drizzled over the top.

Baked Custard Tarts

This recipe is one of my favourites. It is a little more demanding to make but well worth the effort. The filling needs to be prepared the day before.

1 recipe Sweet Pastry (see page 70)

Filling

600ml milk

3 large fresh bay leaves, plus extra to decorate

6 egg yolks (plus 1 extra if eggs are small)

75g caster sugar

1 whole nutmeg

Makes six 6cm tarts

1. To prepare filling, place milk and bay leaves in a saucepan and heat until hot, but not boiling.
2. Meanwhile, place egg yolks and caster sugar in a bowl and beat with an electric mixer until pale and creamy – around 5 minutes.
3. Remove bay leaves and pour milk over egg mixture slowly, stirring well as you pour. Once fully combined, pour into an airtight container and refrigerate overnight.
4. On a lightly floured bench, roll out pastry to 3mm thick and line six 6cm loose-bottom tart tins, trimming pastry to form a neat edge. Rest pastry cases in refrigerator or freezer for at least 30 minutes.
5. Preheat oven to 200°C. Place tray in oven to heat. Pour custard filling into cases, filling to 3mm below the rim. (Do not overfill.) Grate nutmeg over tarts, giving each a generous coating.
6. Place tarts on heated tray and bake for 10 minutes.
7. Lower heat to 180°C, without opening oven door, and bake for another 10 minutes, until filling is set and just golden. Be careful not to over-bake – the custard should be a bit wobbly when tarts are removed from oven.
8. Leave to cool on a wire rack before removing tarts from tins. Decorate each tart with a small bay leaf. Serve at room temperature.

Apple Charlottes

These simple, old-fashioned pies are best made
with Granny Smith apples.

1 recipe Sweet Pastry (see page 70)
8 apples
juice of 1 lemon
125g unsalted butter
¼ cup caster sugar
1 tsp ground cinnamon
seeds of 1 vanilla pod
mascarpone, to serve

Makes six 6cm tarts or one 28cm round tart

1. On a lightly floured bench, roll pastry to 3mm thick and line six 6cm or one 28cm loose-bottom tart tin, trimming pastry to form a neat edge and saving pastry leftovers for the lattice top. Placed lined tins in freezer to rest while preparing apple filling.
2. Preheat oven to 180°C. Place a tray in oven to heat.
3. Peel, core and quarter apples. Cut into 1cm cubes and toss in lemon juice to prevent browning.
4. In a heavy-based saucepan, melt butter and sugar, stirring regularly.
5. Add apple cubes to butter and stir continuously over a medium to high heat. When apple is tender, add cinnamon and vanilla seeds, quickly stir to combine and remove from heat. Leave to cool.
6. Remove pastry cases from freezer and fill with cooled apple.
7. Roll remaining pastry 2mm thick, cut into strips and make a lattice top, trimming edges.
8. Bake on oven tray for 45 minutes for both small tarts or one large tart, or until golden on top and pastry base is cooked through. Leave to cool before removing from tin. Serve with mascarpone.

Kitchen Notes

If you aren't cooking peeled apples immediately, cover in water and lemon juice until ready to use. Try to cut apple cubes a uniform size, so they cook evenly. When cooking the apples, aim for a tender, not mushy, texture.

little and friday.

Mille Feuille

A very popular pastry, which we fill according to the season – in summer we use strawberries; in winter we use poached rhubarb.

1 sheet Flaky Pastry (see page 116)

2 cups Crème Pâtissière (see page 159)

sliced strawberries or 12 pieces Poached Rhubarb (see page 164)

icing sugar, to decorate

Makes 6

1. Roll out Flaky Pastry to 4mm thick on a floured bench. Using a sharp knife, cut into 12 rectangles measuring 15cm × 5cm. Place on two baking trays lined with baking paper and rest in refrigerator for 30 minutes.
2. Preheat oven to 200°C.
3. Cover one tray of pastry rectangles with a sheet of baking paper. These will be the bases of the Mille Feuille. Lay another baking tray over the top of the bases. This will prevent them rising up too much and creating an uneven surface.
4. Bake pastry bases and lids for 10 minutes or until pastry is golden. Allow to cool before assembling.
5. Using a piping bag, spread Crème Pâtissière along the six bases. Divide strawberries or rhubarb between bases.
6. Spread another, thinner layer of Crème Pâtissière over fruit and top with pastry lids. Dust generously with icing sugar. If the stacks tend to topple, they can be tied with a pretty ribbon.

Christmas Mince Tarts

The Fruit Mince mixture should be prepared at least 3 weeks –
and up to 3 months – in advance. The longer it soaks, the better,
but don't let it dry out. Top up with more brandy if needed.

Fruit Mince

1½ cups chopped good-quality dark chocolate

2½ cups sultanas

1 cup raisins

1 cup chopped dates

1 cup chopped prunes

½ cup diced dried apricots

½ cup diced dried pineapple

½ cup mixed peel

2 cups grated apple

1½ cups brown sugar

4 tsp mixed spice

1¼ cups brandy

1 recipe Sweet Pastry (see page 70)

icing sugar, to decorate

Makes 24 tartlets

1. To prepare Fruit Mince, place all ingredients in a large airtight container and stir so fruit is well coated with brandy.
2. Stir every day for at least 3 weeks until ready to use. If you have a food processor, you can lightly pulse mixture to create a finer mince.
3. On a lightly floured bench, roll out pastry to 3mm thick and using an 8cm cookie cutter, or a glass or lid, cut out 24 circles. Line two 12-hole mini muffin trays with pastry, trimming to form a neat edge. Reserve remaining pastry for lids.
4. Rest uncooked pastry cases in refrigerator or freezer for at least 30 minutes, before placing on an oven tray lined with baking paper.
5. Preheat oven to 180°C.
6. Fill pastry cases with Fruit Mince to the rim. Roll out remaining pastry and cut out small stars to place on top of Fruit Mince.
7. Bake for 20 minutes, or until pastry is golden. Allow to cool before removing from tins. Dust with icing sugar to serve.

Kitchen Notes

We use 5cm shallow muffin tins to make bite-sized pies. If making very small pies it can be less messy to put the Fruit Mince in a piping bag and carefully pipe into each case. We've found it to be faster when making large quantities.

little and friday.

Doughs

Little and Friday is famous for its brioche and donuts,
which have my wonderfully versatile Brioche Dough as their
base. Once you've mastered them, try out some of your
own variations and favourite fillings. The dough is also
great for pizza bases.

Brioche Dough

Chocolate Brioche

Cinnamon, Date & Walnut Brioche

Bread & Butter Puddings

Savoury Brioche

Cream Donuts

Cinnamon Donuts

Date & Orange Scones

Brioche Dough

We use this dough for our donuts, stuffed brioche and
Bread & Butter Puddings. In many recipe books you will see
brioche made using the laminated procedure. We have
adapted this recipe so it is easier to make, and I find it is
lighter and fluffier, which is perfect for our donuts.

550ml milk

60g fresh yeast, crumbled, or
3 tsp dried yeast

6½ cups flour

3 tsp salt

½ cup caster sugar

3 eggs

140g unsalted butter

1. In a saucepan, heat milk over a medium heat until
   lukewarm. Remove from heat and sprinkle over yeast. Stir
   until yeast has dissolved.
2. Place dry ingredients into a mixing bowl. Using an electric
   beater with a dough hook attachment, mix at a low speed.
   If you do not have a beater, mix by hand to fully combine.
3. Add yeast mixture and eggs to bowl, continuing to mix at a
   low speed. Mix until a sticky dough forms.
4. Stop mixer and scrape down dough from sides of bowl.
   Increase to medium speed and mix for 10 minutes until an
   elastic, shiny dough forms and pulls away from bowl. If doing
   this by hand, tip dough onto bench and knead for 10 minutes.
5. Cut butter into small pieces and gradually add to dough
   mixture, mixing until well combined.
6. Cover bowl with a tea-towel and allow dough to prove until it
   has almost doubled in size. Tip dough onto a floured bench.
   It is now ready to use.

Kitchen Notes

The proving, or rising, of the dough is highly dependent on the room temperature. Traditionally, brioche recipes require the dough to be chilled overnight or for at least two hours prior to use. I tend to avoid this method as it can make the dough slightly firmer and less fluffy. But this does mean that you have to work faster once the dough is ready, in order to stop it from over-proving, especially during the summer months. If you find it is proving too quickly, you can place it in the refrigerator for short periods to slow down the process. The dough also freezes well.

Chocolate Brioche

These goey treats are at their most delicious fresh out of
the oven, when the chocolate is still melted. Be prepared
to get messy!

1 recipe Brioche Dough (see
page 98)

1 cup Chocolate Ganache (see
page 162)

200g good-quality dark
chocolate (at least 50 per cent
cocoa), chopped

Egg Wash (see page 117)

Makes 9

1. Preheat oven to 180°C. Grease 9 Texas muffin tins.
2. On a floured bench, roll dough into a rectangle measuring
   approximately 45cm × 20cm and 1cm thick. Position dough
   on bench so longer side is facing you.
3. Spread a thick layer of Chocolate Ganache over the dough
   ensuring it is fully covered, and sprinkle over chocolate
   chunks.
4. Roll up dough away from you to form a long log. Using a
   sharp knife, slice into 5cm-wide slices – you should end up
   with nine scrolls. Place each scroll into a muffin tin. Brush
   tops with Egg Wash.
5. Bake for 20 minutes or until golden brown. Allow to cool
   before removing from tins. If melted chocolate leaks out the
   bottoms, spoon it back in so you don't miss out on any of the
   goodness!

Cinnamon, Date & Walnut Brioche

This brioche has a wonderful caramelly flavour and is great for breakfast as it's not too rich.

1 cup walnut halves

1 cup brown sugar

¾ cup dates, finely chopped

75g unsalted butter, diced

1 tbsp ground cinnamon

1 recipe Brioche Dough (see page 98)

Egg Wash (see page 117)

Makes 9

1. Preheat oven to 180°C. Grease 9 Texas muffin tins.
2. Place the first five ingredients in a food processor and blitz until mixture has a coarse breadcrumb consistency.
3. On a floured bench, roll dough into a rectangle measuring approximately 45cm × 20cm and 1cm thick. Position dough on bench so longer side is facing you.
4. Spread a thick layer of walnut mixture over dough, ensuring it is fully covered.
5. Roll up dough away from you to form a long log. Using a sharp knife, slice into 5cm-wide slices – you should end up with nine scrolls. Place each scroll into a muffin tin. Brush tops with Egg Wash.
6. Bake for 20 minutes or until golden brown. Allow to cool before removing from tins. If some of the walnut mixture leaks out the bottoms, spoon it back in.

Bread &
Butter Puddings

These Bread & Butter Puddings are something special.
Chocolate and raspberry is our favorite combination.
You could try using a mix of white and dark chocolate.

2 cups frozen raspberries, or any
other fruit of your choice

½ cup chopped good-quality
dark chocolate

½ cup ground almonds

18 slices stale white bread or
6 brioche, sliced

½ cup sliced almonds, to
garnish

Custard

7 eggs

1 cup cream

2 cups milk

¾ cup caster sugar

½ tsp vanilla essence or paste

Makes 6

1. Preheat oven to 180°C. Grease sides and bottoms of a 6-hole Texas muffin tray and line with baking paper to extend 3cm above the rim of the tins. Layer baking paper in strips to cover sides, so there are no gaps.

2. In a bowl, mix berries, chocolate and ground almonds so fruit is evenly coated with almonds.

3. Using a cookie cutter or glass approximately the same size as the muffin tins, cut a circle from each slice of bread.

4. Place a layer of bread in the bottom of each tin and spoon over a heaped tablespoon of berry mixture. Repeat this process, so each tin has two layers of bread and two of berries.

5. Cut six more discs of bread and cut a small hole in the middle of each, so they look like donuts. Place on top of each pudding, and fill centre with remaining fruit mixture.

6. In a bowl, whisk together custard ingredients. Pour enough custard over each pudding to just cover the top layer of bread. Leave to soak for 20 minutes. Once absorbed, top up with remaining custard mixture.

7. Sprinkle with sliced almonds and cook for 50 minutes, or until puddings are firm to touch. No liquid should seep out.

8. Once cool, remove from tins. These are best eaten immediately, but will keep for up to 3 days in the refrigerator.

Savoury Brioche

A great mid-morning or afternoon snack, these brioches
are popular with customers who need a break from
all the sweet treats.

1 recipe Brioche Dough (see page 98)

½ cup basil pesto

1 cup crumbled feta

1 cup grated vintage tasty cheese

12 sundried tomatoes, chopped

2 cups fresh baby spinach

Egg Wash (see page 117)

Makes 9

1. Preheat oven to 180°C. Grease 9 Texas muffin tins or small tin cans.
2. On a floured bench, roll dough into a rectangle measuring approximately 45cm × 20cm and 1cm thick. Position dough on bench so the longer side is facing you.
3. Spread pesto over dough ensuring it is fully covered. Scatter over feta and tasty cheese, and sprinkle with sundried tomatoes. Lastly, lay a thick layer of spinach over top.
4. Roll up dough away from you to form a long log. Using a sharp knife, slice into 5cm-wide slices – you should end up with nine scrolls. Place each scroll into a muffin tin. Brush tops with Egg Wash.
5. Bake for 20 minutes or until golden brown. Allow to cool before removing from tins.

Cream Donuts

This is our famous donut recipe. Customers queue from 8 a.m. to get their hands on these, and we can easily sell up to 400 on a busy Saturday. We started out making just a dozen, but word quickly spread. These are best enjoyed in private – definitely not a first date experience!

1 recipe Brioche Dough (see page 98)

oil for frying

½ cup Raspberry Coulis (see page 161) or raspberry jam

1 recipe Crème Diplomat (see page 159)

icing sugar, to coat

Makes 15

1. Roll out dough on a floured bench to 4cm thick. Using an 8cm cookie cutter, cut out 15 circles.
2. Allow dough to prove for 10-15 minutes, depending on weather. It will need less time if it is a warm day. You will know it is ready when a dry skin forms on dough.
3. Pour oil into a large saucepan to 2cm deep and heat to 180°C. To cook donuts accurately you need a thermometer. If you are not using one, heat the oil over a medium heat – once it starts smoking it is too hot.
4. Depending on size of saucepan, drop several donuts at a time into hot oil. You do not want them to touch or they will stick together. Cook for 2 minutes on each side. You want dough to be quite dark and crisp. Remove and allow to cool.
5. Once cool, poke a hole into each donut with the handle of a teaspoon to create a cavity.
6. Fill a piping bag with Raspberry Coulis and squeeze 1 tsp into each cavity.
7. Use a clean piping bag to fill cavities with Crème Diplomat – fill each donut until it starts to expand.
8. Dust each donut liberally with icing sugar.

Lemon Curd Donuts

Make donuts as above, using 1 tsp Lemon Curd (see page 160) in place of Raspberry Coulis.

little and friday.

Cinnamon Donuts

Just try and eat one of these without licking
your lips – officially impossible.

1 recipe Brioche Dough (see page 98)
oil for frying
2 cups caster sugar
2 tbsp ground cinnamon

Makes approx. 15

1. Roll out dough on a floured bench to 4cm thick. Using an 8cm cookie cutter, cut out 15 circles. Use a smaller cutter to make holes in the middle of each one. (You can also use a donut cutter available from specialty baking stores.)
2. Allow dough to prove for 10–15 minutes, depending on the weather – it will need less time if it is a warm day. You will know it is ready when a dry skin forms on the dough.
3. Pour oil into a large saucepan to 2cm deep. Heat oil to 180°C. To cook donuts accurately, you need a thermometer. If you are not using one, heat the oil over a medium heat – once it starts smoking it is too hot.
4. Depending on the size of the saucepan, drop several donuts at a time into the hot oil. You do not want them to touch or they will stick together. Cook for 2 minutes on each side. You want the dough to be quite dark and crisp.
5. Mix together caster sugar and cinnamon. Remove donuts from oil and toss immediately in caster sugar and cinnamon.

Kitchen Notes
We use coconut cooking oil – the only healthy thing about these donuts! It's unrefined oil that is very hard to burn, which means we can get our donuts even crispier. At home, as an alternative, use vegetable or canola oil.

little and friday.

Date & Orange Scones

My friend Cheryle Thomas shared this recipe with me,
which was in turn given to her by her mother. The addition
of yoghurt makes the scones lighter.

150ml milk

200ml cream

⅓ cup yoghurt

2½ cups chopped dates

¾ cup self-raising flour

2½ cups plain flour

⅓ cup caster sugar

1 tbsp baking powder

zest of 3 oranges

50g unsalted butter, melted

Egg Wash (see page 117)

½ cup demerara sugar

Makes 6 large scones

1. In a bowl, combine milk, cream, yoghurt and ½ cup chopped dates. Leave to stand for 1 hour.
2. Preheat oven to 180°C. Line an oven tray with baking paper.
3. In a separate bowl, combine flours, sugar, baking powder, zest and remaining chopped dates.
4. Make a well in centre of dry ingredients and pour in milk mixture and melted butter. Gently fold with a large metal spoon or your hands until only just combined. Be careful not to over-mix at this stage or the scones will be tough.
5. Turn dough onto a floured surface and shape into a 5cm-thick rectangle.
6. Using a sharp knife, cut dough into six squares. Place onto lined baking tray.
7. Brush tops of scones with Egg Wash, and sprinkle liberally with demerara sugar. Bake for 15 minutes, then turn tray around and bake a further 15 minutes. Scones are done when they bounce back when lightly pressed.

Savoury Tarts & Pies

Cakes may have been my first love, but during my time in Christchurch I fell in love with pastry too. Mastering it can take some patience and practice, but is so rewarding.

Flaky Pastry

Potato, Blue Cheese & Prosciutto Galettes

Caramelised Onion, Mushroom & Mozzarella Galettes

Walnut Pesto, Leek & Halloumi Galettes

Caramelised Leek, Fig & Venus Cheese Galettes

Ratatouille Pies

Cheese Straws

Bacon & Egg Pies

Mince & Cheese Pie

Sausage Rolls

Steak & Potato-top Pies

Chicken, Leek & Bacon Pie

Frittata

Paprika & Gruyère Pastry

Roast Vegetable Tart

Caramelised Beetroot & Blue Cheese Tart

Quiche Lorraine

Caramelised Onion & Feta Tarts

Flaky Pastry

Making our pastry from scratch gives us the point of difference to many other cafés and results in people queuing out the door on the weekends for our pastries. This pastry is time consuming to make, so if you lack patience you may prefer to buy yours. Two things are key to good pastry. It must be kept cool; so no hot hands or equipment. Plus, the longer you leave your pastry to rest in between rolls and folds, the flakier it will be. We make our pastry a day before we use it.

3 cups flour
pinch of salt
450g unsalted butter, frozen
180ml iced water

Egg Wash
2 eggs
2 tbsp cream

1. Sift flour and salt into a large bowl. Grate 180g butter into bowl and, using your fingers, work into flour.
2. Dice remaining butter into 1cm cubes and add to bowl. Lightly mix with your hands until butter cubes are coated with flour mixture.
3. Add iced water and mix with your hands until dough starts to come together. (The mixture will be studded with large lumps of butter and quite dry at this point.)
4. Tip mixture onto a floured bench and gently work together with your hands to form a rough ball.
5. Roll out to a 30cm × 20cm rectangle. With a long side of the rectangle facing you, fold both short sides to meet at the centre. Then fold in half again.
6. Wrap in cling film and chill in refrigerator for at least 2 hours, or ideally overnight.
7. Roll into a 30cm × 20cm rectangle and fold as before. Do this twice, then return to refrigerator for 30 minutes to rest.
8. Cut pastry in half. Roll each half out to 5mm thick to form two pastry sheets. This pastry does not keep and is best used within 24 hours.

Egg Wash

Place eggs and cream in a bowl and whisk until smooth. You can make as much Egg Wash as you need by using the same ratio of eggs to cream.

Potato, Blue Cheese & Prosciutto Galettes

Good-quality cheese is essential to the success of these galettes. We use local New Zealand cheeses and there are so many good ones to choose from. The better the flavour, the less you need to use – so it is actually quite economical in the end.

1 sheet Flaky Pastry (see page 116)
Egg Wash (see page 117)

Topping
olive oil
2 sprigs rosemary, leaves stripped and finely chopped
5 cloves garlic, finely chopped
4 potatoes, cubed and parboiled
salt and freshly ground pepper
1 cup crumbled blue cheese
6 slices prosciutto
6 sprigs rosemary, to garnish

Makes 6

1. Line two trays with baking paper.
2. On a floured bench, roll out Flaky Pastry to 4mm thick. Using a sharp knife cut six rectangles measuring 10cm × 15cm and place 2cm apart on lined baking trays. When cutting pastry, use a very sharp knife and make a clean cut. Do not drag pastry as it will prevent it from puffing up. Score a line 1cm in from the edge to create a border, taking care not to cut right through pastry.
3. Brush pastry with Egg Wash. Rest pastry cases in refrigerator for at least 30 minutes.
4. Preheat oven to 200°C. Heat enough olive oil to cover the bottom of a frying pan. When piping hot add rosemary and garlic. Allow to infuse briefly before adding potatoes. Sauté until lightly browned.
5. Spoon a small mound of potatoes onto each pastry base, and season with salt and pepper. Bake for about 12 minutes or until golden brown.
6. Crumble a handful of blue cheese over each base before returning to oven to bake until cheese has melted, approximately 3–5 minutes. Top with a slice of prosciutto and garnish with a sprig of rosemary. Serve hot.

Caramelised Onion, Mushroom & Mozzarella Galettes

We recommend making extra quantities of onions and mushrooms to keep on hand for pastas, pizza toppings, antipasto platters – or just to have on toast.

1 sheet Flaky Pastry (see page 116)

Egg Wash (see page 117)

Topping

12 large Oven-roasted Mushrooms (see below)

6 × 5mm-thick slices buffalo mozzarella

1½ cups Caramelised Onions (see page 166)

salt and freshly ground pepper

6 sprigs fresh thyme, to garnish

Makes 6

1. Preheat oven to 200°C. Line a tray with baking paper.
2. Place Oven-roasted Mushrooms on lined tray and top each mushroom with a slice of mozzarella. Bake until cheese is melted or slightly golden. Set aside.
3. On a floured bench, roll out Flaky Pastry to 4mm thick. Using a sharp knife, cut into six rectangles measuring 10cm × 15cm. Do not drag pastry as it will prevent it from puffing up. Score a line 1cm in from the edge to create a border, taking care not to cut right through pastry.
4. Place pastry bases 2cm apart on trays lined with baking paper. Brush pastry with Egg Wash and rest in refrigerator for at least 30 minutes.
5. Spread 2 tbsp Caramelised Onions evenly over each base, inside the scored border.
6. Bake about 12 minutes or until golden brown. Top galettes with mushrooms and melted mozzarella. Garnish with a sprig of fresh thyme. Serve hot.

Oven-roasted Mushrooms

Preheat oven to 250°C. Place 12 large Portobello mushrooms stalk side up on a lined oven tray. Brush with olive oil and sprinkle with chopped fresh rosemary and thyme. Season with salt and freshly ground pepper. Lay a sheet of aluminium foil over the mushrooms and seal tightly. Roast for 7–10 minutes or until mushrooms begin to weep. Set aside to cool.

Walnut Pesto, Leek & Halloumi Galettes

This is our most popular galette topping – we will never take it off our menu. For a very nice variation, replace the halloumi with a good-quality Brie.

1 sheet Flaky Pastry (see page 116)

Egg Wash (see page 117)

Topping

½ cup Walnut Pesto (see page 169)

½ cup Caramelised Leeks (see page 166)

salt and freshly ground pepper

6 × 5mm-thick slices halloumi

12 Oven-roasted Tomatoes (see below)

olive oil

6 sprigs fresh thyme, to garnish

Makes 6

1. Line two trays with baking paper.
2. On a floured bench, roll out Flaky Pastry to 4mm thick. Using a sharp knife, cut into six rectangles measuring 10cm × 15cm. Do not drag pastry as it will prevent it from puffing up. Score a line 1cm in from the edge to create a border, taking care not to cut right through pastry.
3. Brush pastry with Egg Wash. Place pastry bases 2cm apart on lined baking trays and rest in refrigerator for at least 30 minutes.
4. Preheat oven to 200°C. Spread 2 tbsp Walnut Pesto evenly over each base inside scored border.
5. Spoon 2 tbsp Caramelised Leeks on top of pesto and season to taste.
6. Place one slice of halloumi on top of each galette.
7. Bake about 12 minutes or until golden brown. Remove from oven and top each galette with 2 small (or half a large) Oven-roasted Tomatoes and garnish with a sprig of fresh thyme. Serve hot.

Oven-roasted Tomatoes

Preheat oven to 200°C. Place 12 small vine-grown tomatoes, or 3 large tomatoes cut in half, on a lined baking tray (if halved, place cut side up). Drizzle tomatoes with olive oil and season with salt and pepper. Roast in oven for 10 minutes.

little and friday.

Caramelised Leek, Fig & Venus Cheese Galettes

Another variation of our popular galettes. Venus cheese is available from specialty stores, but if you can't get it then blue cheese is a delicious substitute.

1 sheet Flaky Pastry (see page 116)

Egg Wash (see page 117)

Topping

1 cup Caramelised Leeks (see page 166)

6 balls Over the Moon Venus cheese, or 1 cup crumbled blue cheese

6 fresh figs, cut into segments

6 slices prosciutto

2 tbsp olive oil

Makes 6

1. Line a tray with baking paper.
2. On a floured bench, roll out Flaky Pastry to 4mm thick. Using a sharp knife cut six rectangles measuring 10cm × 15cm and place 2cm apart on lined baking tray. Score a line 1cm in from the edge to create a border, taking care not to cut right through pastry.
3. Brush pastry bases with Egg Wash and rest in refrigerator for at least 30 minutes.
4. Preheat oven to 200°C. Spread 2 tbsp Caramelised Leeks evenly over each base, inside the scored border. Place cheese over and top with fig segments.
5. Bake for about 12 minutes. Remove from oven, top each galette with a slice of prosciutto and a drizzle of olive oil, then return to oven for a further 3-5 minutes, until prosciutto has crisped up and pastry is golden brown. Serve hot.

Ratatouille Pies

This ratatouille recipe is from one of our customers.
It works really well topped with lashings of Parmesan
and a flaky pastry crust.

½ cup olive oil

3 cloves garlic

2 tbsp fresh thyme

1 tbsp caster sugar

1 onion, chopped

3 courgettes, chopped

1 red capsicum, sliced

1 eggplant, diced

1 cup black olives

2 cups chopped pumpkin

400g tin chopped Italian
tomatoes, puréed

4 tbsp tomato paste

1 cup water

salt and freshly ground pepper,
to season

2 cups grated Parmesan

1 sheet Flaky Pastry (see
page 116)

Egg Wash (see page 117)

Makes 12 small pies

1. Preheat oven to 180°C. Place all ingredients except
   Parmesan and pastry in a large casserole dish and cook for
   1 hour.
2. Spoon ratatouille filling into 12 × 1-cup ramekins, filling to
   1cm below rim.
3. Sprinkle Parmesan over top.
4. Heat oven to 200°C. Roll pastry to 4mm thick on a floured
   surface. Cut out 12 circles, slightly bigger than top of
   ramekins.
5. Place pastry lids on top of ramekins and brush with
   Egg Wash. Place ramekins on a baking tray and cook for
   10 minutes, until pastry is golden.

Kitchen Notes

For an attractive variation, create a lattice pastry lid for your pies.
Instead of cutting out circles from the pastry, cut strips of pastry.
Weave the pastry strips across the top of the pies in a lattice or
herringbone pattern. Trim edges.

Cheese Straws

These are a weekend only specialty at Little and Friday,
and customers line up early to get 'em while they're hot.

1 sheet Flaky Pastry (see
page 116)
Egg Wash (see page 117)
1½ cups grated tasty cheese
½ cup chopped rosemary
generous pinch of flaky sea salt

1. Preheat oven to 200°C. Line a baking tray with baking paper.
   Lay pastry on a floured bench and paint entire surface with
   Egg Wash.
2. Sprinkle with cheese and rosemary right to edges. Season
   with salt.
3. With a sharp knife, slice pastry into 3cm-wide strips.
4. Grasp both ends of a strip and twist each end in opposite
   directions. Repeat with all strips.
5. Place on lined baking tray, making sure straws are at least
   5cm apart.
6. Bake for 15–20 minutes, or until cheese is melted and pastry
   golden. These need to be eaten the day they are made and
   are at their best still warm from the oven.

Kitchen Notes

To prevent the straws collapsing as the cheese melts, pinch the pastry
together along the length of each straw.

Bacon & Egg Pies

Sunday is Bacon & Egg Pie day at our Belmont store.
We start pulling them out of the oven at 8 a.m. as the first punters roll
in straight out of bed. For many of our regulars, Sunday would not be
the same without a strong coffee and a Bacon & Egg Pie first thing.

1 sheet Flaky Pastry (see page 117)

12 rashers middle bacon, rind removed

1 tomato, cut into 6 wedges

salt and freshly ground pepper

12 eggs

¼ cup cream

Makes 6 small pies

1. Preheat oven to 200°C. Grease a 6-hole Texas muffin tray with cooking spray.
2. Roll pastry to 4mm thick on a floured bench and cut into 9cm squares. Ease pastry squares into muffin tray, being careful not to stretch pastry. Trim edges to form a neat edge 1cm above rim of tray.
3. Line each pastry case with 2 rashers bacon and place a wedge of tomato in each. Season with salt and pepper.
4. Break 6 eggs into a bowl and whisk in cream.
5. Pour egg mixture into each pastry case to one-third full. Gently break a single egg into each filled case, being careful not to break yolks.
6. Place in centre of oven and cook for 25 minutes. Pies are ready when you press down on tops and no liquid seeps out.

Mince & Cheese Pie

Little and Friday's version of this Kiwi classic.

dash of olive oil

1 medium onion, finely chopped

2 cloves garlic, crushed

500g lean beef mince

⅓ cup plain flour

175ml beef stock

salt and freshly ground pepper

1 tbsp tomato purée

2 tsp Vegemite

1 tbsp balsamic vinegar

1 recipe Flaky Pastry (see page 116)

1 cup grated tasty cheese

Egg Wash (see page 117)

Makes 1 large pie

1. Heat oil in a large frying pan, add onion and sauté to soften. Add garlic and cook for 1–2 minutes.
2. Add mince, stirring constantly with a wooden spoon, until browned. Stir in flour and cook for 1 minute.
3. Add half the beef stock, stirring constantly. Once absorbed, slowly add the remaining stock and season with salt and pepper.
4. Stir in tomato purée, Vegemite and vinegar. Simmer for 15–20 minutes on a low heat. Stir occasionally so mince doesn't catch on base of pan.
5. Remove from heat and allow to cool before filling pies, or pastry will go soggy.
6. Preheat oven to 200°C.
7. On a floured surface, roll pastry out to 4mm thick and cut in half. Use one half to line pie dish and trim edges. Allow to rest in refrigerator for 20 minutes. Reserve remaining pastry for lid.
8. Fill pastry-lined tin with mince to the rim. Top pie with grated cheese.
9. Roll remaining pastry for lid.
10. Paint rim of pastry-lined tin with Egg Wash. Lay pastry lid on top and firmly press down on the edges with your fingers. Trim overhanging pastry with scissors or a sharp knife. Using a knife, pierce the centre of pie several times.
11. Glaze lid with Egg Wash and bake for 25 minutes or until golden brown.

Sausage Rolls

Voted the best sausage roll in Auckland by *Metro* magazine,
these are so good because of the organic meat and homemade pastry.
Tradition demands that they are eaten with a good tomato sauce.

1kg sausage meat

¼ cup Tomato Relish (see page 168)

1 heaped tbsp fresh thyme, chopped

½ cup grated Parmesan

1 sprig fresh rosemary, stripped and chopped

salt and freshly ground pepper, to season

1 sheet Flaky Pastry (see page 116)

handful of fresh basil or baby spinach leaves, plus extra basil leaves to garnish

Egg Wash (see page 117)

Makes 6

1. Preheat oven to 200°C. Line two baking trays with baking paper.
2. Using your hands, combine sausage meat, Tomato Relish, thyme, Parmesan, rosemary and salt and pepper in a large mixing bowl.
3. Roll out pastry to a rectangle measuring about 30cm × 24cm. Cut in half, so you have two 30cm × 12cm rectangles.
4. Arrange one piece of pastry so long side is facing you. Place half the meat mixture along pastry edge closest to you to form a tidy log. Lay half the basil on top of meat.
5. Paint a line of Egg Wash along other long pastry edge.
6. Roll up pastry to enclose meat tightly. Repeat with other piece of pastry and remaining filling. Cut each log into three even-sized pieces and place seam-side down on prepared baking trays.
7. Score tops of sausage rolls twice with a sharp knife. Brush tops and sides of each roll with Egg Wash and decorate with a single basil leaf. Bake for 20 minutes or until golden brown.

Kitchen Notes

In summer, we use fresh basil in our sausage rolls. In winter, we use spinach as basil can be expensive.

little and friday.

Steak &
Potato-top Pies

These classic pies can be frozen and reheated straight
from the freezer at 180°C for 20 minutes.

1 sheet Flaky Pastry (see
page 116)

Filling
dash of olive oil

1kg beef steak, cut into 2cm
pieces

4 onions, roughly chopped

2 cloves garlic, finely chopped

4 rashers bacon, chopped

3 tbsp fresh thyme

1½ cups red wine

2½ cups beef stock

salt and freshly ground pepper

2 tbsp cornflour

3 tbsp water

Topping
4 large Agria potatoes,
quartered

3 tbsp cream

knob of unsalted butter

salt and freshly ground pepper

Egg Wash (see page 117)

Makes six 9cm pies

1. Preheat oven to 180°C. Grease six 9cm pie tins.
2. To prepare filling, heat olive oil in a large frying pan and
   sauté steak, small portions at a time to prevent stewing.
   Transfer to a large casserole dish.
3. Sauté onions and garlic until golden. Add to casserole dish
   with bacon, thyme, red wine and stock. Season with salt and
   pepper, cover and cook in oven for 1 hour.
4. Mix cornflour and water to form a paste. Stir through meat
   mixture until fully combined.
5. Return casserole to oven for 30 minutes, until meat is tender
   and mixture is thickened. Leave to cool before filling pies, or
   pastry will become soggy.
6. To prepare topping, boil potatoes in salted water. Drain and
   add cream, butter, salt and pepper. Mash and set aside to
   cool.
7. On a floured surface, roll pastry out to 4mm thick and
   cut into 15cm squares. Ease pastry into prepared tins.
   Do not trim edges. Allow pastry to rest in refrigerator for
   20 minutes.
8. Preheat oven to 200°C. Place tray in oven to heat.
9. Fill lined tins with steak mixture to the rim. Using an ice
   cream scoop or tablespoon, roll a large ball of potato and
   place on top of steak filling.
10. Fold overhanging corners of pastry around mash to form a
    tight seal. Paint mash and pastry with Egg Wash.
11. Place pies on tray in centre of oven and cook for 25 minutes
    or until pastry is golden.

little and friday.

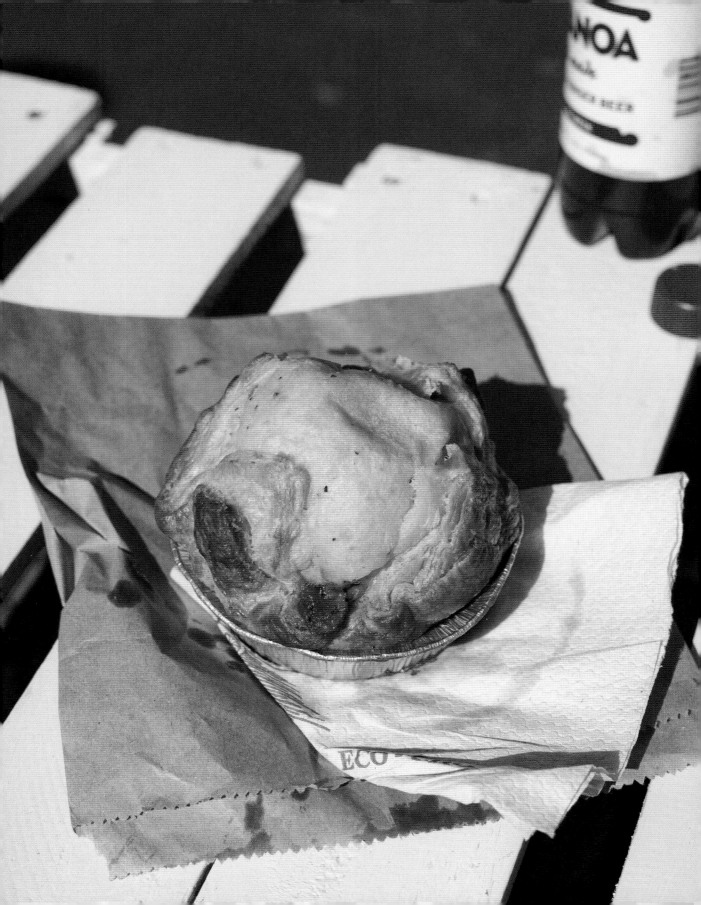

Chicken, Leek & Bacon Pie

Another winter classic, the addition of bacon and cheese makes this pie extra hearty and rich.

1 recipe Flaky Pastry (see page 116)

Filling

75g unsalted butter

4 rashers streaky bacon, chopped

1kg chicken thigh fillets, cut into 2cm pieces

4 leeks, chopped

½ tsp thyme

⅓ cup flour

3½ cups chicken stock

1 tbsp Dijon mustard

½ cup Italian parsley, chopped

salt and freshly ground pepper

1 cup grated Gruyère

Egg Wash (see page 117)

Makes 1 large pie

1. Grease one large or six 9cm round pie dishes.
2. On a floured surface, roll pastry to 4mm thick and cut in half, reserving one half for lattice top. Use other half to line pie dish. Allow to rest in refrigerator for 20 minutes.
3. Melt butter over a medium-high heat. Sauté bacon until just browned. Set aside.
4. Add chicken to pan and brown for approximately 4 minutes. Set aside.
5. Lower heat, add leeks and thyme to pan and soften. Set aside.
6. Add flour to remaining butter in pan to form a roux. Cook for 2 minutes, stirring constantly. Slowly add chicken stock, one cup at a time, to create a thick sauce.
7. Add chicken, bacon and leeks to sauce. Cook for 20 minutes over a medium heat, stirring occasionally to prevent sauce from catching. The mixture should be thick enough for the chicken and leeks not to sink to the bottom. Add mustard and parsley and season with salt and pepper. Set aside to cool.
8. Preheat oven to 200°C. Fill pastry-lined pie dish with chicken filling to the rim. Top with grated cheese.
9. Cut remaining pastry into thin strips for lattice lid.
10. Paint pastry-lined rim of pie with Egg Wash. Lay pastry strips across pie filling and firmly press with your fingers to seal edges. Trim overhanging pastry with a sharp knife. Glaze pastry with Egg Wash and bake in oven for 25 minutes or until golden brown.

little and friday.

Frittata

We started making these savoury cakes in response to requests from coeliac customers, who loved our sweet gluten-free treats but could not eat anything savoury. You could add bacon or prosciutto to the recipe. Any leftover egg mix makes delicious scrambled eggs.

3 cups baby spinach

olive oil

1 sprig rosemary, stripped and chopped

5 cloves garlic, finely chopped

3 large Agria potatoes, parboiled and cubed

1 cup Caramelised Leeks (see page 166)

4 Oven-roasted Courgettes (see page 146)

2 red and 2 yellow capsicums, chargrilled and sliced into strips

1 cup chopped sundried tomatoes

1 cup grated Parmesan

1 cup crumbled feta

½ cup vegetable relish

12 eggs

⅓ cup cream

salt and freshly ground pepper

Makes one 25cm × 15cm frittata

1. Preheat oven to 180°C. Line the bottom and sides of a 25cm × 15cm loaf tin with baking paper, ensuring the lining extends 10mm above the rim and is fully enclosed to prevent leakage.
2. Arrange baby spinach in a thick layer over the base and sides of the tin to form a nest.
3. Heat sufficient olive oil to cover the bottom of a frying pan. When smoking-hot, add rosemary and garlic. Allow the oil to infuse briefly then add potatoes to the frying pan and sauté until lightly browned. Scatter potatoes over spinach in the tin.
4. Layer remaining vegetables and cheeses in the tin, spooning dollops of vegetable relish throughout.
5. Whisk together the eggs and cream until combined. Pour mixture carefully into the tin up to the rim and season with salt and pepper.
6. Bake for 50 minutes or until the surface springs back to the touch. Allow to cool completely before removing from the tin, as the frittata will collapse if still hot.

Kitchen Notes

Any sort of vegetable relish or chutney is good to add flavour. We use Ajvar mild vegetable relish, which is a capsicum-eggplant blend.

Paprika & Gruyère Pastry

This pastry can be frozen in the tins. Thoroughly cover pastry-lined tins in cling film and freeze. When required, simply remove the cling film and fill; you do not need to defrost the pastry first.

75g unsalted butter
1¼ cups flour
½ tsp paprika
½ tsp mustard powder
½ cup grated Gruyère
salt and pepper
1 egg yolk
2 tbsp iced water

Makes one large tart or six 6cm tarts

1. In a bowl, rub butter into flour until mixture resembles fine breadcrumbs.
2. In a separate bowl, mix together paprika, mustard powder, Gruyère and salt and pepper. Mix in egg yolk and water.
3. Add cheese mixture to flour and lightly knead together to form a soft dough.
4. Wrap in cling film and rest in the refrigerator for at least 30 minutes before using. This pastry keeps well in the refrigerator for up to a week. Use leftover pastry to line extra tins, which can be wrapped in cling film and frozen until needed.

little and friday.

Roast Vegetable Tart

*This is most definitely a summer tart – add eggplants
or artichokes if in season.*

1 recipe Paprika & Gruyère
Pastry (see page 144)

Filling

1 cup grated Parmesan

½ cup crumbled feta

2 tbsp basil pesto

8 chargrilled red and yellow
capsicums, finely sliced

salt and freshly ground pepper

10 Oven-roasted Courgettes
(see below)

18 Oven-roasted Tomatoes
(see page 122)

8 Oven-roasted Mushrooms (see
page 120)

Makes one 12cm × 35cm tart

1. Grease a 12cm × 35cm loose-bottom tart tin.
2. On a floured bench, roll pastry out to 3mm thick and line tin.
   Place on an oven tray and refrigerate at least 30 minutes.
3. Preheat oven to 180°C. Spread Parmesan and feta over
   pastry case. This creates a seal that prevents pastry from
   going soggy.
4. Spread pesto over cheeses and cover with sliced capsicum.
   Season with salt and pepper.
5. Roll slices of courgette around your finger into tight spirals.
   Pack tightly into pastry case, spiral side up, until full.
6. Bake for 30 minutes or until pastry is golden. Leave to
   cool before removing tart from tin. Top with Oven-roasted
   Tomatoes and Oven-roasted Mushrooms.

Oven-roasted Courgettes

Preheat oven to 180°C. Cut courgettes lengthwise into 3 mm
slices. Place on a tray lined with baking paper and lightly coat
with olive oil or canola oil spray. Season with salt and freshly
ground pepper and roast for 15 minutes or until soft and cooked
through.

Caramelised Beetroot & Blue Cheese Tart

To make these you need a really good blue cheese for flavour.
Roasting the beetroot is a bit time consuming but if you make extra
beetroot it is great tossed through salads with good feta and walnuts.

1 recipe Paprika & Gruyère
Pastry (see page 144)

Filling

1 cup grated tasty cheese

1 cup crumbled blue cheese

salt and freshly ground pepper

3 cups baby spinach

1 recipe Caramelised Beetroot
(see page 166)

12 eggs

⅓ cup cream

Makes one 28cm round tart

1. Grease a 28cm loose-bottom tart tin with butter or cooking
   spray.
2. On a floured bench, roll out Paprika & Gruyère Pastry to
   3mm thick. Line base and sides of prepared tin, trimming
   edges. Rest in refrigerator for at least 15 minutes.
3. Preheat oven to 180°C. Place tart on a lined oven tray.
   Sprinkle unbaked pastry case with tasty cheese and top with
   crumbled blue cheese.
4. Season with salt and pepper, then scatter spinach over
   cheese.
5. Arrange wedges of Caramelised Beetroot in a spiral, starting
   from the outside and working in.
6. Combine eggs and cream in a jug and pour into pastry case
   to 2mm below the rim. Try to pour mixture underneath
   spinach leaves. Don't let egg mixture overflow or tart will
   stick in tin.
7. Bake in centre of oven for 50 minutes, until egg mixture is
   set. Check by pressing gently on top of the tart; if no liquid
   seeps out it is ready.

little and friday.

Quiche Lorraine

I found a bundle of old recipe books dating back to 1911
at a Christchurch flea market. This tart is adapted from a
recipe found in one of these books. It is a simple, old-fashioned
recipe that uses good-quality bacon for flavour.

1 recipe Paprika & Gruyère
Pastry (see page 144)

Filling

2 tbsp wholegrain mustard

1 cup grated tasty cheese

1 cup finely chopped onion

1 cup finely chopped parsley

2 cups finely chopped organic
bacon

salt and freshly ground pepper

14 eggs

½ cup cream

6 Oven-roasted Tomatoes (see
page 122), to garnish (optional)

Makes one 12cm × 35cm tart

1. Grease a 12cm × 35cm loose-bottom tart tin with butter or
   cooking spray.
2. On a floured bench, roll out pastry to 3mm thick. Line
   base and sides of prepared tin, trimming edges. Rest in
   refrigerator for at least 15 minutes.
3. Preheat oven to 180°C. Place tart case on an oven tray. Mix
   mustard through cheese and sprinkle over pastry. Top with
   onion, parsley and bacon. Season with salt and pepper.
4. Whisk together eggs and cream until combined. Carefully
   pour egg mixture into pastry case to 2mm below the rim.
   If egg mixture overflows the tart will stick in tin.
5. Bake for 50 minutes, until egg mixture is set and top is
   golden. Check this by pressing gently on top of tart; if no
   liquid seeps out, it is ready. Leave to cool before removing
   tart from tin. Garnish with Oven-roasted Tomatoes, if
   desired.

Caramelised Onion & Feta Tarts

These are the first tarts I made and they have never left
the menu. They still prove to be the most popular tarts we make.

1 recipe Paprika & Gruyère
Pastry (see page 144)

Filling

1 cup grated tasty cheese

2 cups crumbled feta

3 cups Caramelised Onions (see
page 166)

salt and freshly ground pepper

12 eggs

⅓ cup cream

Makes six 6cm tarts or one 28cm round tart

1. Grease six 6cm or a 28cm loose-bottom tart tin.
2. On a floured bench, roll out Paprika & Gruyère Pastry to
   3mm thick. Line base and sides of prepared tins, trimming
   edges. Rest in refrigerator for at least 15 minutes.
3. Preheat oven to 180°C. Place lined tins on an oven tray.
   Sprinkle with tasty cheese and crumbled feta and top with
   Caramelised Onions. Season with salt and pepper.
4. Whisk eggs and cream together until combined. Carefully
   pour egg mixture into pastry case to 2mm below rim. If egg
   mixture overflows tart will stick in tin.
5. Bake for 35 minutes for small tarts or 50 minutes for a large
   tart in centre of oven until egg mixture is set and top is
   golden brown. Check by pressing gently on top of tart; if no
   liquid seeps out, it is ready. Leave to cool before removing
   from tin.

Finishings & Fillings

These things are great to have on hand. You can make them well in advance as they all keep well.

Candied Lemon Zest, Orange Peel & Carrots

Frangipane

Cream Cheese Icing

Crème Pâtissière

Crème Diplomat

Lemon Curd

Raspberry Coulis

Caramel

Chocolate Ganache

Chocolate Spirals

Poached Pears, Rhubarb & Tamarillos

Caramelised Onions, Leeks & Beetroot

Tomato Relish

Tamarillo Chutney

Walnut Pesto

Candied Lemon Zest

6 lemons, coarsely zested
2 cups caster sugar

1. Place zest in a saucepan with enough cold water to cover and bring to the boil.
2. Drain, then repeat this process.
3. Place cooked zest and sugar in a pan with enough cold water to cover and bring to a boil. Reduce heat to low and simmer until the zest is almost translucent. Keep checking water level to make sure it doesn't boil dry.
4. Remove from heat and leave to cool. Store zest and juices in an airtight container for up to 2 weeks.

Candied Orange Peel

peel of 10 oranges
3 cups caster sugar

1. Place orange peel in a saucepan with enough cold water to cover and bring to the boil.
2. Drain, then repeat this process.
3. Place orange peel and 2 cups sugar in saucepan with enough cold water to cover and bring to the boil. Reduce heat to low and simmer until the peel is almost translucent. Keep checking water level to make sure it doesn't boil dry.
4. Remove from heat, drain and leave to cool. Transfer orange peel to a tray lined with baking paper and leave to dry overnight.
5. The following day, dip the pieces of orange peel in the remaining 1 cup caster sugar to coat. Store in an airtight container for up to 2 weeks.

Candied Carrots

3 carrots
3 cups caster sugar

1. Peel carrots in long strips as thick as you can get with a peeler. They need to be as long as the length of the carrot, and thick enough to stop them from breaking into smaller pieces.
2. Place strips in a saucepan with enough cold water to cover, add caster sugar and bring to the boil. Turn heat down and simmer until translucent – this can take up to 2 hours. Keep checking the water level to make sure it doesn't boil dry.
3. Remove from the heat and leave to cool. Store carrot in sugar syrup in an airtight container for up to 2 weeks.

Kitchen Notes
Candied fruits and vegetables should not be stored in the refrigerator, as we find this crystallises the sugar.

Frangipane

125g unsalted butter, softened
½ cup caster sugar
2 eggs
1½ cups ground almonds
1 tbsp flour

Makes 2 cups

1. Cream butter and sugar with an electric mixer until light and fluffy. Stop the beater and scrape the sides of the bowl frequently to ensure ingredients are being thoroughly combined.
2. Add eggs one at a time and beat well. Ensure first egg is well integrated before adding the next.
3. Using a wooden spoon, stir in ground almonds and flour to form a paste. Frangipane will keep in an airtight container in the refrigerator for up to 2 weeks.

Cream Cheese Icing

125g unsalted butter, softened and cubed
500g cream cheese, cubed
1 cup icing sugar, sifted

Makes 3½ cups

1. Thoroughly cream butter in an electric mixer on high speed, continuously scraping down sides of bowl.
2. Soften cream cheese by squeezing through your fingers and add to butter. Continue beating on high until there are no lumps, scraping down sides of bowl frequently.
3. Turn mixer to slow speed and add sifted icing sugar. When icing sugar is fully integrated, turn up speed and beat until mixture is smooth. Refrigerate in an airtight container for up to 2 weeks.

Crème Pâtissière

500ml milk
1 tsp vanilla essence or paste
½ cup caster sugar
3 egg yolks
¼ cup cornflour

Makes 2½ cups

1. In a saucepan, combine milk, vanilla and ¼ cup caster sugar, and bring to the boil.
2. In a separate bowl, beat together remaining caster sugar, egg yolks and cornflour until pale and thick.
3. Slowly pour half the milk mixture into egg mixture, whisking constantly.
4. Return remaining milk to the heat. When it has reached boiling point, quickly add egg yolk mixture, whisking constantly. As you add egg mixture to milk it will cool slightly. Keep whisking combined mixture vigorously over heat until it returns to the boil, then remove from heat.
5. Pour into a bowl and lay a circle of baking paper on top so it does not form a film on surface.
6. Refrigerate in an airtight container for up to 3 days. Beat the crème until smooth before using, as it will form a solid mass once chilled.

Crème Diplomat

150ml cream
½ recipe Crème Pâtissière (see above), chilled

Makes 2½ cups

1. Whip cream until firm.
2. Beat chilled Crème Pâtissière until smooth. Fold gently through whipped cream with a metal spoon. Refrigerate in an airtight container for up to 3 days.

Lemon Curd

125g unsalted butter
1 cup caster sugar
juice and zest of 4 lemons
3 large eggs

Makes 2 cups

1. Place all ingredients except eggs in a metal bowl. Place bowl over a saucepan of simmering water and stir until sugar has dissolved completely. You can check this by rubbing a small amount of cooled mixture between your fingers. It is not ready if the consistency is still granulated.
2. Remove from heat. In a separate large metal bowl, beat eggs with an electric mixer. Add butter and sugar mixture to eggs and beat until combined.
3. Pour mixture though a strainer to remove zest.
4. Place mixture back over simmering water and cook slowly until thick enough to coat a spoon. Refrigerate in an airtight container for up to 3 weeks.

little and friday.

Raspberry Coulis

4 cups raspberries, fresh or frozen

¼ cup caster sugar

¾ cup water

juice of 1 lemon

2 tbsp cornflour

2 tbsp water

Makes 2¼ cups

1. Place berries in a large saucepan. Add sugar, water and lemon juice and bring to a simmer.
2. Blend cornflour with water to make a smooth paste and add to berries.
3. Bring mixture to the boil, stirring constantly to prevent it catching on the bottom. Cook for 5 minutes. Refrigerate in an airtight container for up to 4 weeks.

Kitchen Notes

This mixture can also be blended to make a purée. However, we prefer to keep the fruit chunky to add texture to our donuts, cakes and meringues.

Caramel

2 cups caster sugar

600ml cream

Makes 3 cups

1. Place sugar in a small saucepan and just cover with water to achieve a wet sand consistency.
2. Bring to the boil but do not stir. Using a wet pastry brush, clean down sides of saucepan to remove any stray sugar crystals.
3. Continue to boil until the sugar turns amber. At this point, quickly remove from heat.
4. In a small saucepan, heat cream to boiling point. Gradually add this to caramelised sugar, stirring constantly to achieve a smooth consistency. This may take a while but it will eventually combine.

Kitchen Notes

Timing is paramount with Caramel. Both the cream and the sugar need to be really hot when they are combined.

Chocolate Ganache

200g good-quality dark chocolate (we use 50 per cent cocoa)
½ cup cream

Makes 1 cup

1. Gently melt chocolate and cream in a metal bowl over a saucepan of simmering water. Stir constantly to form a smooth sauce.
2. Allow to cool and thicken. Store in a cool place for up to 2 weeks.

Kitchen Notes

You can make as much Ganache as you need by using the same ratio of chocolate to cream. In cold weather you may need to use ¾ cup cream. Ganache may also need to be warmed slightly before use.

Chocolate Spirals

1 cup cooking chocolate

Makes approx. 50

1. Place chocolate in a metal bowl over a saucepan of simmering water. Do not allow bottom of bowl to touch water or chocolate will burn. Melt slowly, stirring frequently.
2. Carefully fill a piping bag with melted chocolate. On a lined baking tray, pipe spiral shapes approximately 5cm in diameter.
3. Allow to set at room temperature, depending on the weather. In hot weather refrigerate for a short time. The spirals will keep for a long time in a cool place.

Kitchen Notes

Don't use good-quality chocolate for this recipe as it will not set. The key to piping spirals is not to put too much chocolate in the bag. Twist the top of the bag tight to create downward pressure on the melted chocolate.

Poached Pears

6 green pears, peeled and cored
2 star anise
2 cinnamon quills
1 tbsp manuka honey
1 cup caster sugar

Makes 6

1. Place enough water in a large saucepan to cover pears and bring to the boil.
2. Add star anise, cinnamon quills, honey and caster sugar. Stir until sugar has dissolved, then add pears.
3. Simmer for 30 minutes, or until pears have softened and become transparent but retain their shape. Remove from saucepan, reserving liquid, and allow to cool. Pears can be refrigerated in an airtight container with their liquid for up to 5 days.

Kitchen Notes

To prevent the pears discolouring while cooking, make a *cartouche*. Before cooking the pears cut a circle of baking paper to fit the circumference of your saucepan. Cut a hole in the centre of the circle to allow some of the steam to escape. Lay the paper on the surface of the water while the pears are cooking, pressing down every so often to make sure the steam is released.

Poached Rhubarb

5 stalks rhubarb
juice and zest of 3–5 oranges
1–2 cups caster sugar
¼ cup orange blossom water

Makes approx. 20 pieces

1. Preheat oven to 180°C.
2. Cut rhubarb stalks into 8cm-long pieces and place in a deep baking dish.
3. In a bowl, combine orange juice and zest, sugar and orange blossom water. Pour over rhubarb and toss to coat.
4. Bake for approximately 20 minutes or until tender, turning occasionally. Cool and store in an airtight container in the refrigerator.

Poached Tamarillos

12 tamarillos
juice and zest of 5 oranges
2 cups caster sugar

Makes 12

1. Preheat oven to 180°C. Boil a large saucepan of water.
2. Using a sharp paring knife, score the skin of the tamarillos into quarters lengthwise.
3. When water is at a rapid boil, drop tamarillos into water for approximately 2 minutes, or until the skin peels away from the fruit. Drain.
4. Peel skin off tamarillos and place on a baking tray.
5. Combine orange juice, zest and sugar, and stir through tamarillos.
6. Bake for approximately 20 minutes, turning regularly, until rich in colour.

Kitchen Notes

Don't allow tamarillos to sit in hot water once their skins have peeled back. This will make them waterlogged.

The number of oranges you need will depend on how juicy they are. You want the fruit to be almost completely covered in liquid while cooking in the oven. If you skimp on orange juice, the rhubarb will become woody and dehydrated, and the tamarillos will be too caramelised.

Caramelised Onions

Makes 4 cups

8 large onions, peeled and finely sliced
4 tbsp balsamic vinegar
6 tbsp brown sugar

1. Place all ingredients into a large saucepan over a high heat and stir frequently.
2. When onions begin to brown and liquid reduces, lower heat.
3. Remove from heat when onions turn dark brown.
4. Store in an airtight container in the refrigerator for up to 2 weeks.

Caramelised Leeks

Slice 2 leeks in half lengthwise. Cut leaves crosswise to 5mm thickness. Heat enough olive oil to coat the bottom of a frying pan. When piping hot add prepared leeks and sauté, taking care not to overcook. Season to taste with salt and freshly ground pepper. Add a knob of butter and remove from heat. Makes 2 cups.

Caramelised Beetroot

Makes 6 cups

6 large beetroot
2 tbsp balsamic vinegar
3 tbsp brown sugar

1. Preheat oven to 180°C.
2. Cut off beetroot tops and cut each beetroot into 6 wedges. Place in a saucepan and cover with salted water. Boil for about 10 minutes or until soft.
3. Drain, reserving 2 cups of cooking liquid.
4. Spread beetroot out on a baking tray. Pour over reserved liquid and balsamic vinegar and sprinkle with brown sugar.
5. Bake for 10 minutes. Remove from oven and baste with liquid in tray. Bake for a further 10–20 minutes, basting as necessary, until liquid has reduced and beetroot is sticky.

Tomato Relish

2.7kg tomatoes, skins and all, chopped

1kg onions, finely chopped

2 cloves garlic, chopped and crushed

600ml white wine vinegar

2 tbsp wine vinegar

2 cups sugar

1 tbsp salt

½ tsp chilli powder

1 tsp ground ginger

1 tsp mustard powder

salt and freshly ground pepper

Makes 12 cups

1. Combine all ingredients in a saucepan on a medium heat.
2. Season to taste with salt and freshly ground pepper and cook for approximately 2 hours, stirring occasionally, until thick and pulpy.
3. Store in the refrigerator.

Tamarillo Chutney

1.75kg peeled tamarillos

5 green apples, peeled and chopped

3 large onions, chopped

3 cups malt vinegar

1 tsp salt

1½ tsp mustard powder

1 tsp mixed spice

4 cups brown sugar

Makes 10 cups

1. In a large saucepan, combine all ingredients and bring to the boil.
2. Reduce heat and simmer for 2 hours. Store in the refrigerator.

Walnut Pesto

1 cup walnut halves
4–6 cloves garlic, peeled
2 handfuls curly parsley
2 tbsp olive oil
salt and freshly ground pepper

Makes 2 cups

1. Place walnuts, garlic and parsley into the bowl of a food processor and blend until combined but still coarse.
2. With the motor running, pour in olive oil. Add just enough oil to combine – the mixture should be dry and not overly oily. Season to taste.
3. Store in an airtight container in the refrigerator for up to 1 week.

Helpful Hints

Essential equipment, ingredients, techniques and tips to
help you with the recipes in this book.

Mixing

We use a food processor for making all of
our pastries and some biscuits not requiring
aeration. If you don't have one, elbow
grease is just as good but a little harder and
more time consuming! We never use a food
processor for making cakes, as the mixture
needs to have air beaten into it; a food
processor cannot achieve this. Cakes must be
mixed by hand or with an electric beater.

Oven Temperatures

The temperatures stated in this book are for
fan bake, which are usually lower by about
10–20°C than temperatures for conventional
ovens. Using fan bake helps to move air
around the oven, so you can cook several
cakes at once.

All ovens are different; older models in
particular can vary. You may need to get
your thermostat checked if you are finding
recommended cooking times consistently
inaccurate. It's a good idea to check baked
goods 10 minutes before the recommended
cook time.

Lining Tins

To grease tins, you can melt butter and
brush it over the inside of the tin. We use
cooking spray, which is a lot faster. To help
cakes come out even more cleanly we use
baking paper cut to fit the bottom of the tin
and line the sides. It is a little more fiddly but
worth the extra preparation time as the tins
are also easier to clean.

Filling Tins

Once baking soda or powder is added to wet
ingredients it starts working immediately.
Because of this, you want to get your mixture
in the oven as soon as possible once these
ingredients are added. Any tin should not be
filled to more than two-thirds full. Make sure
to spread the batter evenly so it is flat.

Baking Cakes

Ideally cakes should be placed in the centre
of the oven. If you are baking several cakes
at the same time, try to give them space so
the air can circulate around the oven. If they

are on separate shelves, don't place them directly over each other. When checking on your cakes, open and close the oven door gently – do not slam it. It is better not to open the oven at all during the first quarter of the baking period.

A Clean Hand

I find my hand is the most useful tool in the kitchen (make sure that it is clean, though – I find I wash my hands about 50 times a day). When you use your hand in place of a spoon or spatula you have more understanding of the mixture because you can feel it. It is a slower process, which gives you more control and means you are far less likely to over-mix.

Eggs

We use size seven eggs. I highly recommend free range for baking as they create a much nicer cake. Make sure to bring eggs to room temperature before using.

When you are combining eggs and sugar, make sure to mix them straight away. Do not leave them to sit as the sugar will burn the egg yolks. Meringues and macaroons work better with older eggs (around 10 days old) than fresh.

Beating Egg Whites

Bring eggs to room temperature and ensure bowl and beater are clean and dry. There are three stages that the eggs will go through: the first is foam; then soft peaks; and finally firm peaks. The peaks are found by dipping in your finger and pulling it out – a stiff peak should hold its form. At the soft-peak stage they will not hold their points and droop over.

Chocolate

For baking we use 50 per cent cocoa solids, nothing less, as it will definitely alter the cake's flavour. Chocolate should be stored at room temperature in a dry, airtight container. Be careful to keep it away from strong flavours such as onions or spices as it will absorb their flavour. To melt chocolate, place in a stainless-steel or glass bowl over a pot of simmering water. Do not allow the bottom of the bowl to touch the surface of the water as it will burn and seize.

Caster Sugar

We use caster sugar in all of our baking because it dissolves more quickly and easily.

Unsalted Butter

Bakers only ever use unsalted butter and add salt separately to taste. Like chocolate, it should be kept in an airtight container away from strong flavours. Make sure to bring it to room temperature before using.

Creaming

When creaming butter and sugar, bring the butter to room temperature and cut into cubes. Using an electric mixter, beat until the texture is smooth and fluffy. There should be no grains of sugar left in the mixture.

Flour

For all pastry, we use high-grade flour. It is higher in protein (gluten), which strengthens the pastry. We use plain flour for our cakes and biscuits.

Index

Acknowledgements

Firstly, my biggest thank you has to go to my right arm, my backbone: Holly. When we began she was only 15, and ended up leaving school way too early to help create the look, design and everything that Little and Friday is. She would come with me before the sun rose, sacrificing her social life as well as her sleep to fulfil our dream.

Secondly, to my mum and dad for their continuous support over the years, helping me achieve my dream when everyone else said I couldn't. To Dad for arriving from Tauranga with his boot full of tools ready to repair or alter anything that needed attending to in the shop. To Mum for hours of sewing aprons and cooking chutneys to sell.

To all the people who have passed through the doors at L & F: the ones who have worked here; bought food here; emptied their cupboards of treasures for us to use; and those who have harvested their gardens to bring us fresh produce and flowers along the way.

To all those who believed in L & F and supported our organic crazy growth, especially Debra Millar of Penguin, who has had immense patience as I continually overrode the deadlines.

Thanks to Rosie, Elle and Julia for helping me get my recipes and ideas out of my head and down onto paper.